Praise for *Most Dangerous Women*

Most Dangerous Women presents history in a way that will transform students or others who perform or watch it into active learners, giving them a sense of "you are there."
> —Dr. Merry Wiesner-Hanks, professor of history, UW–Milwaukee
> and author, *Gender in History*

This is indeed most dangerous history, global stories of courage representing a buried current of hope. I'd love to see students all over the country performing it in their classes.
> —Paul Loeb, author of *Soul of a Citizen: Living with
> Conviction in a Cynical Time*

Readers who undertake to enact this play will find themselves carried away by the depth of insight, extraordinary strength of will, and the rugged tenacity of each woman, and for one brief moment will be elevated in imagination and courage to see the world as they did.
> —Dr. Rosalie M. Romano, Ohio University, author of *Forging an
> Educative Community* and *Hungry Minds in Hard Times*

The book includes Maher's play (coauthored with Nikki Nojima Louis), the story of women's international peace efforts from 1918 to the present, incorporating period music, speeches, and newspaper headlines. It offers practical classroom suggestions not just for bringing this play to life but for creating an original work on any social movement.
> —Wendy Ewbank, president, Washington State
> Council on the Social Studies

Most Dangerous Women is a handbook for social studies teachers, complete with key themes, research and discussion questions, and language arts connections. For anyone who's ever flirted with the notion of turning an idea into a play, *Most Dangerous Women* breaks down the process in such a sensible, instructive way that it will surely turn many of its readers into writers.
> —Jo Cripps, teacher, Summit K–12, Seattle, Washington

I am deeply moved by this work, and honored to have my words included in *Most Dangerous Women.*
> —Amber Amundson, cofounder Peaceful Tomorrows
> (an organization founded by family members
> of those killed on September 11)

This text provides teachers with a solid foundation for bringing the particular history of the women of WILPF to life in the classroom or the theatre. And it offers techniques for history teachers to create their own scripts to enliven other areas of the curriculum.

—Dr. Bobbi McKean, Theatre Education and Outreach, School of Theatre Arts, University of Arizona

Jan Maher has done it again—she weaves together compelling historic material and the creative methods she has developed as a teacher and performer. She leads us to deeper understanding and more effective teaching about the enduring issue of peace.

—Mary Hammond Bernson, University of Washington

This book is a treasure—not only the script, which tells the story of the unsung heroines and heroes of the peace movement, but also in the very helpful step-by-step process of bringing this story to a live audience.

—Joanne Dufour, adjunct faculty, Heritage University

Jan Maher's creative, yet pragmatic suggestions provide me with a wonderful toolkit to deliver content in a way that reaches both the minds and the hearts of my students. This book should be on the shelf of any high school teacher who teaches in the inner city.

—Victoria Bernstein, teacher, Cleveland High School, Seattle, Washington

Most Dangerous Women made me proud to be a woman. Girls like me from all over the world made a difference, and now I know I can, too. The book gave me the facts that were left out in all my other history books at school.

—Kayla Liederbach, high school student, Waukesha, Wisconsin

By using quotes from many of the Women's International League for Peace and Freedom's past heroes and orators, the authors of the *Most Dangerous Women* play have created an exciting vehicle for making the history of the past ninety years come alive. They have proved that given the right treatment, the historical record itself is dramatic, and need not be tampered with.

—Margaret Hope Bacon, author of *One Woman's Passion for Peace and Freedom: The Life of Mildred Scott Olmsted*

A more effective means of educating the public about the role of women in fostering world peace could hardly be imagined.

—Dr. Craig Eisendrath, Senior Fellow, Center for International Policy, Washington, D.C., coauthor (with Helen Caldicott) of *War in Heaven*

Most Dangerous Women
Bringing History to Life Through Readers' Theater

Jan Maher

HEINEMANN
Portsmouth, NH

Heinemann
A division of Reed Elsevier Inc.
361 Hanover Street
Portsmouth, NH 03801–3912
www.heinemann.com

Offices and agents throughout the world

The author and publisher wish to thank those who have generously given permission to reprint borrowed material:

Photograph of the First International Congress at the Hague courtesy of Records of the Women's International League for Peace and Freedom, Swarthmore College Peace Collection.

Excerpts from *Most Dangerous Women: Feminist Peace Campaigners of the Great War* by Anne Wiltsher. Copyright © 1985. Published by Pandora Press. Reprinted by permission of the literary estate of the author.

Excerpts from *Pioneers for Peace: Women's International League for Peace and Freedom 1915–1965* by Gertrude Bussey and Margaret Tims; London: British Section: WILPF. Reprinted by permission.

Credits continue on page vi

Library of Congress Cataloging-in-Publication Data
Maher, Jan.
    Most dangerous women : bringing history to life through readers' theater / Jan Maher.
      p. cm.
    Includes bibliographical references.
    ISBN 0-325-00910-4 (alk. paper)
    1. Readers' theater. 2. Drama in education. 3. History—Study and teaching. 4. Women pacifists—Juvenile drama. 5. Peace movements—Juvenile drama. I. Title.
    PN2081.R4M34 2006
    808.5'45—dc22   2005031524

Editor: Danny Miller
Production coordinator: Sonja S. Chapman
Production service: Aaron Downey, Matrix Productions Inc.
Cover photo: Courtesy of a postcard from Helaine Victoria Press, Inc.
Cover design: Night & Day Design
Compositor: Valerie Levy / Drawing Board Studios
Manufacturing: Jamie Carter

Printed in the United States of America on acid-free paper
10   09   08   07   06   ML   1   2   3   4   5

I want strong peace.
—Muriel Rukeyser

For all of history's peacemakers.

Contents

Acknowledgments

There are so many to thank. Three who must top the list are Sylvia Lundt, unfortunately no longer with us, whose request to Nikki Nojima Louis for "a little something" to celebrate the 75th anniversary of the Women's International League for Peace and Freedom (WILPF) led to the play *Most Dangerous Women*; Nikki, who invited me to work with her to research and develop the project; and Joan Szymko, our music director/arranger. Without Sylvia, Nikki, and Joan there would have been no play; without the play, there would be no book about it. I cannot thank them enough.

Thank you to the many women and men, both members of WILPF and others, who have helped organize productions of *Most Dangerous Women* over the years. They wrote grants and press releases, hosted committee meetings and potlucks, sold tickets, donated money, facilitated auditions, put us up in their homes, and helped in countless other ways. To list them personally would be both to fill pages and to risk leaving someone out. They live in and around Seattle, WA; San Jose, CA; Chicago, IL; Bryn Mawr, Philadelphia, and Swarthmore, PA; Athens, WV; Portland, OR; and Milwaukee and Waukesha, WI. Their enthusiasm for the play is what has kept it alive and growing for some fifteen years.

I must thank, too, the performers: another long list of wonderful women (and a man or two) in all these communities whose presence has infused each performance with wit, compassion, integrity, and authenticity.

Thank you to the many contributors to the script: amazing women and men whose lives were and are continual testaments to the possibility of peace. Thank you to the members of Seattle WILPF, staff at the national WILPF office, and at WILPF's international headquarters in Geneva who assisted us in our research.

Thank you to three generations of "dangerous women" and men in my own family. My mother Alberta Ruth Lang, my sister Diana Maher, and my daughter Rachelle Ackerman inspire me. Each has believed in *Most Dangerous Women* and always encouraged my work on it, as has Allen Lang, my father. My sons, Noah and Joshua Ackerman, represent to me all the sons of all the mothers who have worked to save their children from the horror of war.

My partner, husband, friend for life Doug Selwyn is my best critic, my closest collaborator. His very presence brings me peace.

Thank you to Danny Miller, whose belief in this book and its importance is what has brought it to life, and to Sonja Chapman and Aaron Downey who saw it through to print.

Foreword

Harriet Hyman Alonso

Nikki Nojima Louis and Jan Maher have written a beautiful play that evokes the passion and commitment of various women who have dedicated their lives to achieving world peace. *Most Dangerous Women*, a combination of emotional music, passionate statements, and a strong sense of social justice, is based on the history of two strands of women's peace activism—the work of the organization the Women's International League for Peace and Freedom (WILPF) and the work of individual women who received the Nobel Peace Prize in honor of their dedication to humankind.

WILPF, which is still a vital force in peace efforts, has its roots in the international woman suffrage campaign of the late nineteenth and early twentieth centuries. When the women of the International Woman Suffrage Alliance were unable to hold their biennial meeting in Germany in 1915 because of World War I, a group of European women decided to call a meeting at The Hague instead, with the intention of coming up with a plan for ending this specific war and all wars. That meeting, which is the centerpiece for *Most Dangerous Women*, took place from April 28 to May 1. There were more than a thousand women at the meeting. Most represented the neutral nations, and logically, most of them were from the Netherlands. However, there were numerous representatives from the belligerent nations as well, including six from Austria, twenty-eight from Germany, three from Great Britain, ten from Hungary, and one from Italy. Out of that meeting, which was chaired by Jane Addams of the United States, emerged the International Committee of Women for Permanent Peace whose membership pledged to meet at the end of the war at the same time in the same place as the leaders of the then warring nations. In 1919, national leaders met at Versailles outside of Paris. The women were barred from that area and so met again in Zurich, Switzerland, where they officially formed the Women's International League for Peace and Freedom with headquarters in Geneva, where the League of Nations hosted several of its international conferences.

Most Dangerous Women features several of the women who attended the historic meeting at The Hague. Most well-known was Jane Addams who was asked to chair the meeting because of her international reputation as a settlement house worker and founder of Hull House in Chicago. Addams's work was respected by women (and men) worldwide. Her writings on peace, social justice, and reform were heralded by philosophers, religious leaders, social workers, peace activists, and political leaders. In fact, Theodore Roosevelt, a great admirer of Addams, requested that she second his nomination for the 1912 presidential campaign, a deed she happily took on even though women in the United States did not have the right to vote until 1920. Because Addams was known for her gentle but powerful leadership style and lived in a neutral nation, the International Congress of Women at The Hague requested that she guide the new peace effort. She remained an effective leader and proponent of WILPF's work until her death. In 1931, she received the Nobel Peace Prize for her work with the organization.

Emily Greene Balch was in many ways Addams's right-hand woman in the international WILPF work. Balch attended the 1915 Hague meeting and joined in on the creation of WILPF, staying in Geneva for several of the group's formative years as the secretary-treasurer. Balch had a similar background to Addams's. She had begun her professional life as a social worker but had then turned to the study of economics, which she taught at Wellesley College in Massachusetts for 21 years until she was fired for her anti-war activism during World War I. Although she devoted her life to WILPF, she also wrote many articles on the effects of war on the economy and the environment. In 1946, she, too, was awarded the Nobel Peace Prize for her work with WILPF.

Other women who attended the Hague meeting are featured in *Most Dangerous Women*. Alice Hamilton, physician, medical activist, and friend to Jane Addams, saw herself as tagging along out of devotion to her friend. However, the congress moved her to action, and she became a lifelong voice against war. Anita Augsburg, a German feminist, who along with her partner, Lida Gustava Heymann, worked for various women's causes in Germany, fled the Nazis after their rise to power. Both women continued their efforts from Switzerland. Aletta Jacobs, the Dutch physician who opened the first birth control clinic in the Netherlands, was actually the guiding force behind the organization of the conference. It was she who called together the organizing committee, who saw that money was raised and local arrangements made. She was joined in her effort by Rosa Genoni, one of the few Italian women who was able to attend the congress. And finally, there was the fiery Rosika Schwimmer from the Austrian-Hungarian empire. Schwimmer was one of the most colorful women in the World War I peace movement. She had a flamboyant style and a feisty spirit, and sometimes proposed seemingly outrageous actions, which usually took shape. One was the creation of three delegations of women from the Hague Congress who traveled throughout Europe visiting various countries' leaders and putting forth the women's peace plans.

The work of the women who met in The Hague in the spring of 1915 when the tulips were in full bloom has continued to this day. Their message to the world that nations should negotiate before shooting, that weapons development and sales should be internationally regulated, that people of nations should have the right to determine their nationalities and their style of government, and that women should have the vote and equal rights the world over are issues around which women still organize. *Most Dangerous Women* gives various examples of the work that women have taken on since 1915 through the words and music of such dynamic activists as Hanan Ashwari, Edith Ballantyne, Helen Caldicott, Shirin Ebadi, Coretta Scott King, Gertrude Mongella, Holly Near, Mildred Scott Olmsted, and Nafis Sadik. Their efforts represent the global nature of women's peace activism today.

Most Dangerous Women also utilizes the prestige of the Nobel Peace Prize to emphasize the work of various women. The prize, first presented in 1901, was created from money left in Alfred Nobel's will for the explicit purpose of setting up the various Nobel prizes. In 1905, Bertha von Suttner became the first woman to receive the prize. Interestingly, it was von Suttner's brief relationship as secretary to Nobel and then her correspondence with him concerning her work with the Austrian Peace Society that inspired him to create the prize in the first place. It took 26 years for the prize to be awarded to another woman—Jane Addams—and 15 more until Emily Greene Balch was awarded hers.

Although women are not consistently awarded the Peace Prize, several have received it in recent years, and most of these are present in *Most Dangerous Women*. In 1976, Betty Williams and Mairead Corrigan received the award for efforts to mediate the tensions in Northern Ireland. Mother Teresa was honored in 1979 for her great humanitarian work and in 1982, Alva Myrdal for her antinuclear activism. In 1991, Aung San Suu Kyi of Myanmar was awarded the prize for her efforts for self-determination and human rights as was Rigoberta Menchú Tum the next year. In 2003, Shirin Ebadi received the prize for her work on behalf of women's and children's rights in Iran, and in 2004, Wangari Maathai was the first person ever to receive the prize for work on ecology and economic development. All of these women demonstrate how universal are the issues of women, and how global. For women, peace is not simply the absence of war, it is also economic, political, and social justice. A world at peace is a world of equality and humanity.

The discussion of teaching methods and materials that appear in this volume make *Most Dangerous Women* accessible to children and adults alike. This is a most worthy project, one which gives to educators historical knowledge, educational instruction, and a lesson in heroism, dedication, and action.

Harriet Hyman Alonso is the author of *Peace as a Women's Issue: A History of the U. S. Movement for World Peace and Women's Rights, The Women's Peace Union and the Outlawry of War, 1921–1942*, and the award-winning *Growing Up Abolitionist: The Story of the Garrison Children*. She also wrote the introduction for a reprint of *Women at The Hague: The International Congress of Women and Its Results* by Jane Addams, Emily G. Balch, and Alice Hamilton. Alonso is Professor of History at the City College of New York and the Graduate Center of the City University of New York.

Introduction
Stories That Need Telling

The founders of WILPF at the Hague, 1915

Who are the women of WILPF, and why are they so dangerous (and important)? When my colleague Nikki Nojima Louis and I began to write *Most
Dangerous Women* in 1990, it was because we'd been asked by a member of
the Seattle branch of the Women's International League for Peace and Freedom (WILPF) to "put together a little something" for their 75th anniversary
celebration. We'd barely heard of the organization, but were willing to do
some research. The more we read, the more we were struck by the truth of
the words WILPF founder Rosika Schwimmer said of the gathering that gave
birth to WILPF, "when you realize what did happen, you will realize that this
congress was one of the greatest things that women ever achieved." Throughout the first part of the twentieth century, WILPF was the predominant
women's peace and justice organization in the world. Despite the loss of so

many European members during World War II, WILPF persisted; and in 1953 the organization's importance was recognized when it was granted consultative status at the United Nations.

In the 60 years since Hiroshima, WILPF has continued to be a voice calling for reason, peace, and social justice. Several of the women who have won the Nobel Peace Prize have been members of WILPF. There are, of course, many other organizations that have worked for peace that deserve mention (see Appendix B for a partial list). But one can only do so much in a single play. Even as we've updated the script, we've decided to keep our focus primarily on WILPF, because WILPF is the oldest continuously existing women's international peace organization (the same age as Fellowship of Reconciliation, which deserves at least a play of its own). We've woven in a secondary focus on the women who have won the Nobel Peace Prize.

There is an old saw in playwriting that holds the more particular the story details, the more universal the truth that can be revealed. By attending to this particular organization, the Women's International League for Peace and Freedom, we can consider a whole range of universal truths and questions about peace and war, patterns of international conflict, gender roles, economic justice, and individual courage.

What happened to peace?

Open just about any history book, and you will find plenty of references to war. Indeed, a reasonable sentient being from outer space, browsing a selection of world and U.S. history textbooks, might conclude that war is an essential part of what defines the human race. And a reasonable young person growing up in our educational system might conclude that war is inevitable. Ask history teachers pressed for time how much they covered during their teaching year, and often they will tell you they "only got to the Civil War," or "barely got to World War II," or "didn't have time to teach the Vietnam War, let alone the Gulf War or the war in Iraq." Years in which wars are not the predominant reality are referred to as "between the wars."

And what do the textbooks teach us of these wars, even if we do have time to cover them? In one typical text, there are 24 pages devoted to World War I. Less than the equivalent of one page among them discusses anti-war sentiment prior to U.S. entry into the war. There is no discussion whatsoever of opposition to war in World War II. Little or no mention is made of efforts to avert war through negotiations. Terms of peace settlements are rarely included or given short shrift, and there is little or no discussion of connections between those terms and what happens next in and between the previously warring countries.

In the index, there are no entries for "peace," other than the "Peace Corps" and "Peaceful Coexistence" (referring to the United States and the former Soviet Union during the Cold War), and three mentions of pacifism. Two of these are for William Penn and the Quakers during the American Revolution. The third is a brief mention of opposition to World War I.

But there are a total of more than 115 full pages of war entries. Within those pages, discussion of causes of war is simplified in the extreme, and much of the attention is on specific battles, campaigns, and weapons. Very little attention is devoted to the effects of war on people and on the environment.

It is a very safe bet, however, that the overwhelming majority of ordinary citizens of the world, if asked, would say they prefer peace to war. Wouldn't it make sense, then, to begin to devote some of our instructional time in our history classrooms to the study of peace? Not peace simply as the absence of war, but "the imagination of peace," as the poet Denise Levertov wrote in "Making Peace," her eloquent paean to the role of poets, "an energy field more intense than war." Peace as an expression of the understanding articulated by Joy Harjo, that in wars "there are never any winners" and that without just settlements, future wars are inevitable.

There's another peculiarity of history texts. Women are a majority of the world's population, but garner a minority of the mentions in the books. They are sprinkled throughout, somewhat like the seasoning in the stew. They are not "mainstream" in the story. Rather, they appear in specific roles: Supporting war efforts is large among them. Betsy Ross gets credit for sewing flags, even if it turns out she wasn't the original designer. Nurses such as Florence Nightingale are mentioned for tending the wounded. Rosie the Riveter usually gets a sidebar, and the "firsts" may earn a mention now and then for setting a sports record (Wilma Rudolph) or gaining elective office (Jeannette Rankin).

But there are other stories to tell. They are not in the history texts, not even written "between the lines." One such story is the story of women (and men) who have organized efforts to stop war, to address the root causes of war, to insist that war is neither necessary nor tolerable. As one early peace activist, Mary Sheepshanks, put it: "It is not enough for women to do relief work. We must use our brains to urge peace among unvindictive lines, leaving no cause for resentments such as lead to another war."

A few of the women who are part of this story make it into the history books, but generally not for their peace activism. Jane Addams, for example, is widely mentioned as the founder of Hull House, but rarely mentioned as the first American woman to win the Nobel Peace Prize. Jeannette M. Rankin may be mentioned as the first woman to be elected to the Congress but that she cast her very first vote against U.S. entry into World War I, was the sole vote in the House of Representatives against U.S. entry into World War II, and led a march on Washington calling for withdrawal of our troops from Vietnam is not generally included. Martin Luther King Jr. is widely celebrated for his leadership in the Civil Rights Movement but rarely studied for his opposition to war in Southeast Asia.

Most Dangerous Women tells this story. From the international efforts during World War I to influence governments to end that ghastly conflict to the current calls to end conflicts in various parts of the world, women have been on the front lines waging peace.

Women have a unique perspective on war. Though not all women have children, it can be guaranteed that all soldiers have mothers. And mothers, generally speaking, want to see their children survive. Indeed, if it wasn't an overriding urge of mothers to see their children survive, the species would die out—as would any. It's really a law of nature.

Important Questions

There are a multitude of important questions embedded in the generalities of war in our recorded history. Is war a male impulse, or more inclusively part of human nature? If so, what of the claims that the archeological record shows long periods—lasting upward of 10,000 years—when peace seems to have prevailed in much of the inhabited earth?

Will men and women ever see eye-to-eye about combat? And if they do, will that eye-to-eye become "an eye for an eye," which Mahatma Gandhi once noted will make the whole world blind?

What will happen as more women join the ranks of the armed forces in the United States? Which will change more: the nature of the armed forces or the nature of women? Already people have seen the shocking images of prisoner abuse at the Abu Ghraib prison in Iraq, where the women were seemingly full participants in horrific practices that offended friend and foe alike. Barbara Ehrenreich, speaking to the 2004 graduating class at Barnard College, articulated the dismay well:

> These photos turned my stomach—yours too, I'm sure. But they did something else to me: they broke my heart. I had no illusions about the United States mission in Iraq, but it turns out that I did have some illusions about women.... What we have learned, once and for all, is that a uterus is not a substitute for a conscience; menstrual periods are not the foundation of morality.

In Congress there is debate over whether and how women in the armed forces ought to be assigned to combat zones, or if in this age of terrorism, one can even distinguish a combat zone from a noncombat zone. These questions of gender are crucial ones, in some respects far beyond the scope of this book. And yet, they are what this book is about. From at least as long ago as the fictional Greek heroine Lysistrata to the anti-war activists of the twenty-first century, women have questioned the wisdom of war with anguish, passion, indignation, anger, and intelligence. The voices of many of these women comprise the chorus of *Most Dangerous Women*. There is a male voice or two as well, for peacemaking is not solely the province of women, any more than warmaking is the exclusive province of men. So the focus is primarily on women peace activists in the twentieth and twenty-first centuries, but also on the call for peace in general.

Why is this story of peace activism so compelling and important? We live in an age in which the threat of nuclear war is again increasing. North Korea has announced itself as a nuclear power. The United States is ramping up its nuclear program again. Others are said to want to develop nuclear weapons as well as nuclear power. The Doomsday Clock, set by the Board of Directors of *Bulletin of the Atomic Scientists* to reflect the level of risk of an all-out nuclear disaster, was moved up again to seven minutes until midnight.

Added to the risk of nuclear confrontation is the risk of continuing or new conventional wars, with the inevitably resulting civilian casualties. The United Nations High Commission on Refugees reported that in 2004 there were 17.1 million people who were refugees, asylum seekers, and internally displaced persons.[1] Tens of millions of others were also affected by wars currently smoldering or raging across the globe, for war conditions disrupt lives even when people don't flee their homes. Infrastructures are compromised; disease rates increase exponentially. Relief aid to victims of the tsunami disaster of December 2004 was hampered in areas where there were armed conflicts, most notably around Banda Aceh in Indonesia. Thirty years of conflict between the Free Aceh Movement and the Indonesian military hampered attempts to distribute aid, because each side in that conflict wanted to assert authority in the region. Meanwhile, the people continued to suffer.

It is often the children who suffer most. In 2004, 42 percent of the total population of Iraq, for example, was under the age of 15. In Afghanistan, the percentage was over 43 percent. In Liberia, where there had been 14 years of civil war, it was nearly 47 percent. In the Palestinian territories, over 46 percent of the population was under the age of 15.[2] Rampant disease added to political unrest is even deadlier. In Zimbabwe, in 2005 repressive government and civil strife disrupted the lives of citizens who buried one in every eight children before they turned 5; 70 percent of those lives were lost to AIDS, which also left one in five children in Zimbabwe without parents.[3] Life expectancy in Zimbabwe was expected to continue to drop over the next decade, possibly as low as 27. A 2005 report by the Food and Agriculture

Organization identified armed conflicts as the leading cause of world hunger, and warned that food emergencies are increasingly human made. The report stated that peace is "a public good and an essential condition for attaining the Millennium Development Goals."[4]

By contrast, countries that have been at peace for several decades clearly enjoy the benefits. In Australia, France, Germany, England, and Sweden the percentage of the population that was under 15 in 2004 ranged from 15 to 20 percent, and the life expectancy was 78 to 80. Even Cuba and China fared well in these charts, with life expectancy at 76 in Cuba—just one year lower than the United States—and 71 in China. The country with the longest life expectancy (82), Japan, is one whose very constitution forbids war.[5] The political systems vary widely from country to country, but the correlations between peace and longevity on one hand, and war, disease, and early death on the other holds true the world over.

Given these disturbing statistics, isn't it time we studied peace? Not the Orwellian "war is peace" logic that lasting peace comes through crushing military force or perpetual war, but the kind of peace advocated by the women of *Most Dangerous Women*. These women looked deeply at issues of war and have seen connections to issues of social justice, economic justice, and racial and ethnic justice. They have given us ways to think about how to create social structures that will mitigate against war and support sustainable peace. The *Bulletin of the Atomic Scientists* agrees that something fundamental must change.

> We therefore fully support the statement circulated by *Bulletin* sponsor John Polanyi and signed by 110 Nobel laureates last December, which reads in part, "The only hope for the future lies in cooperative international action, legitimized by democracy. . . . To survive in the world we have transformed, we must learn to think in a new way."[6]

We owe it to ourselves, to our students, to our shared future, to include peace in our study of history. This would be learning to think in a new way. *Most Dangerous Women* is one place to start.

Notes

1. United Nations High Commissioner for Refugees statistics page, retrieved at www.unhcr.ch/cgi-bin/texis/vtx/home?page=statistics.

2. *2004 World Population Data Sheet*, Population Reference Bureau Data Finder, retrieved at www.prb.org/datafind/datafinder5.htm.

3. Zimbabwe: AIDS kills Zimbabwe child every fifteen minutes—UNICEF, Reuters, March17, 2005, retrieved at www.aegis.com/news/ads/2005/AD050498.html.

4. *Armed Conflicts Leading Cause of World Hunger Emergencies*, FAO report, presented at 31st Session meeting of the Committee on World Food Security, 2005, retrieved at www.fao.org/newsroom/en/news/2005/102562.

5. *2004 World Population Data Sheet*, Population Reference Bureau Data Finder, retrieved at www.prb.org/datafind/datafinder5.htm.

6. *Bulletin of the Atomic Scientists*, retrieved at www.thebulletin.org/media/current.html.

1

Working with Most Dangerous Women *in Classroom and Community Settings*

How to Read *Most Dangerous Women*

There's no rule that says you can't simply sit down in your favorite chair, read the script, and leave it at that. Or ask students or friends to do the same. But there are several ways you can enhance the experience. Depending upon your purpose, you may wish to organize a read-around, either for a community group or a classroom, or you may want to make a project of staging *Most Dangerous Women*—again, either as a classroom project for a school audience or with a community theater cast for a general audience. Here are some suggestions for each approach. (These approaches work for any Readers' Theater text that you may wish to explore.) Remember that if you plan to produce *Most Dangerous Women* for a public audience, you will need to secure performance permission. See page 61 for information on whom to contact.

Read-Arounds

The simplest way to structure a reading (beyond a single reader reading the text to her- or himself) is as a read-around. This format expands or contracts to accommodate however many people are reading the play.

The basic format for a read-around is very simple. The participants sit where they can see and hear each other (ideally in a circle, though realistically sometimes a classroom doesn't permit rearranging of chairs). Sound and light cues (such as "*Sound: artillery fire, building to a pitch; then, suddenly, silence*") may be read as lines or omitted. Each person reads the narrative or speech that comes next when it is his or her turn to read. In sections where a named character speaks more than once, several readers may end up sharing the character's lines. On particularly long monologues, two or three

9

readers share the speech. This approach has some distinct advantages, especially in a mixed-gender group. It sets the tone and expectation that it doesn't matter what gender the reader is and that anyone can read any part. What matters is the content of the text.

A slight variation on this structure is to set the convention that the first person to read a named character's line reads all that character's lines through a section in which the character speaks more than once. This can get a bit complicated because that person will be reading out of the established order at times.

Setting a Context

If you are using the text in a classroom, you may want to begin by asking some contextualizing questions that relate the text to the students' prior knowledge. For example, you might ask: How many people know something about World War I? How many people know how people communicated across oceans in 1914? How they traveled between Europe and the Americas? How many people know if they have a grandparent, great grandparent, or great great grandparent who served in the military either in the U.S. or in another country during World War I? How many people know if their ancestors lived in any of the countries that were at war in Europe or in any of the countries under colonial rule of European nations, before the United States entered the conflict? How many remember what their textbook said about the causes of World War I?

Note: it is not necessary to tie a reading of the script to the contents of a specific textbook, but virtually all world history and American history textbooks will have a chapter on the Great War. They will vary in terms of the specifics they emphasize, but all will tend to identify general causes for the war such as the rise of nationalism and militarism in European countries, the historical grievances and mistrusts lingering from earlier wars, the wish of many ruled by large empires for independence, the formation of alliances, and the competition for world markets. All will mention the assassination of the crown prince of the Austro-Hungarian empire, Archduke Francis Ferdinand, as the triggering event that began the sequence of showdowns and ultimatums that led to war. In terms of U.S. involvement, all will mention the German torpedoing of the Lusitania and other noncombatant vessels with American civilians aboard.

If you are in a community setting, the same sorts of questions apply. The general ideas above may or may not be common knowledge, depending upon the group. You will need to decide how important this general background is. One approach is to make sure to review it before reading the play;

an alternative is to let the curiosity and appetite for that background information grow out of the experience of reading the script.

In the classroom, you will probably find that it makes sense to break the reading down into at least two, and possibly four or five, sessions. In a community group, you can read the entire script in one or two sittings. The first act takes approximately 45 minutes to read, and the second approximately 60 minutes.

If you do take more than one session to read through the script, take time to review the previous reading before launching into the next section. What were the key ideas and events of the previous section? What questions do they raise about what is going to happen next? Were there surprises? Things we didn't know about before we began reading? What was the most memorable part of what has already been read?

What about the Songs?

The songs are an important part of *Most Dangerous Women*. Music varies the pace of the reading, making it more interesting. A song can summarize historical content, capture the mood of an era or a particular monologue, or reflect our emotional response to the material. You might want to locate recordings of as many of the songs as you can, in order to be able to play them at the appropriate times during the reading. (See Appendix F for some available sources.) Some of the songs are well-known, and especially in a community group, there may be people who already know some of the songs and are comfortable singing, especially if there's someone around with a guitar or piano backing them up.

If you want to take time to learn some of the songs before the read-through, you can find several of them on CDs or tape, and a few of the songs are available to listen to on the Internet. (See Appendix F section for specific sources.) Be aware that Internet sources may not be authorized to provide downloads. All music sites should have guidelines about whether it is legal to download the music, and if so, for what purposes. Two songs are in the public domain; "Johnny I Hardly Knew Ya" and "Siph' A Mandla N'kosi," so listening to the way a particular group or individual has recorded them can give you some ideas about how to pace and sing them, should you choose to include singing as part of your reading. You can also find the original rendition of "I Didn't Raise My Boy to Be a Soldier," which has additional lyrics to the ones used in *Most Dangerous Women* as well as a different tune.

If gathering some or all of the music is not feasible, don't skip reading the lyrics. Encourage whoever is reading not to rush, but to give the lyrics the same energy that a poem—or for that matter any monologue—deserves.

Discussing the Play after the Reading

Some questions that can guide a debriefing discussion after the play has been read include:

> How many of the names in the play were familiar prior to reading it?
>
> How many of the historical events were known prior to reading it?
>
> What were some of the most surprising things participants learned from the reading?
>
> What are some of the ways women have attempted to influence public opinion and policy over the decades with regard to war and social justice issues?
>
> Which of the monologues, songs, and headlines were most powerful and why?
>
> What are the patterns that seem to repeat through the decades? (Encourage contrasting responses.)
>
> Were there parts of the play that anyone found particularly gratifying to read because she or he already agreed with the point of view expressed?
>
> Were there parts of the play that anyone found difficult to read because he or she saw a situation very differently than the point of view expressed?
>
> What are questions you would most want to research that were raised by the reading?

See Chapter Two for a list of suggestions for further discussion and research.

Staging the Play in an Educational Setting

When I think of all the different objectives that can be accomplished by theater projects in the classroom, an old joke from a vintage *Saturday Night Live* routine spoofing product claims comes to my mind: "It's a floor wax! It's a dessert topping! It's a floor wax *and* a dessert topping!" A few of the teaching objectives that I've observed/experienced are:

- Unskilled readers rarely enjoy reading simply for the sake of practicing reading. But having a role to play gives readers a rationale for reading the same passages over and over, practicing for fluency.

- Students who work together on a performance project develop important social skills. The "show must go on" ethic calls them to much higher expectations for themselves and others.

- Often, students who struggle in other areas excel when it comes to theater. Doing projects that call out their strengths allows them to shine, increasing their self-esteem and their status in the group.
- Performing for an audience is tremendously reinforcing.
- Multiple points of view are inherent in a theater production. Being able to view an issue from multiple points of view is a key social studies skill.

If you choose to do a staging of the play for an audience beyond the participants in the reading, this section offer some specific suggestions.

Casting

If you are performing the play for an audience, it is important to assign character roles that carry through the play. The audience doesn't have a script to follow. Jane Addams, Rosika Schwimmer, Emily Greene Balch, and Jeannette Rankin have lines in a number of different places in the script, so each of these roles should be read by the same person throughout. These actors should have other lines assigned such that it is clear when they are the above named characters and when they are taking other roles. This is a fairly simple matter of not giving them other lines within a section in which their character is appearing.

Give some thought, too, to the qualities your cast members exhibit. Rosika Schwimmer is a role that should go to someone who is able and willing to be forceful. The person playing Jeannette Rankin must be able to capture the comic elements of her lines as well as the serious ones. Coretta Scott King needs to be read with dignity and maturity, Helen Caldicott with dynamic energy, and so forth.

The Rehearsal Process

There are four distinct elements to a rehearsal process for a staged reading of *Most Dangerous Women* (or any other documentary Readers' Theater that includes music) that each merit their own rehearsal time. The first is monologue rehearsal, that is, working with the individual actors on their assigned monologues. The second is music rehearsal, which includes rehearsal of the solo pieces and small ensemble pieces, and whole cast rehearsal of the songs that everybody sings. The third element is whole cast rehearsal in which you work specifically on all the elements that require the attention of the full cast, such as entrances, exits, pacing, the general stage picture, and so forth. Finally, there is tech rehearsal, which is when you do what is called a "cue to cue" rehearsal, with particular emphasis on all the sound and light cues.

Figure 1–1. *Jeannette Rankin appears throughout the play.*

Actors working on monologues (also solo and small ensemble songs) should figure out answers to a number of questions that will help them more fully project the meaning of the material.

- Who is the audience? To whom is the actor speaking? This differs from one monologue to the next. In one sense, they are all directed to the contemporary audience, the one sitting in seats watching the play. But most are also directed in some other way. Jane Addams, in Act I, is reporting back to an audience in the United States as a *New York Times* correspondent who is also a major figure at the First International Congress speaking directly to delegates. So some of her lines ("The large floor is completely filled. . . . .") are by way of explaining the scene to her readers back home. Others ("I find it a pleasure and an inspiration. . . . ") can be directed as well to the delegates assembled in The Hague (i.e., the actor's fellow performers seated on the stage). Mildred Scott Olmsted's story in Act I was told some time after the fact to an interviewer. The actress delivering that monologue is in a very different time and space than would be the case if the piece were written as the story was actually unfolding. Another such monologue is Toyomi Hashimoto's remembering the bombing of Nagasaki. She is looking back on the event rather than living it. At the beginning of Act II, seven actresses give voice to a poem written during a women's peace encampment, directed to a stereotypical male detractor, but very likely for the benefit of like-minded feminists. It's probably best for the actresses to avoid focusing the poem's anger on the men who might be in the audience, who we hope can be presumed to be supportive of the play and its contents. Helen Caldicott's monologue, on the other hand, is a *direct* challenge to *all* the audience to make a serious, life-changing commitment to the cause of peace. Mairead Corrigan Maguire's "Dear Luke" monologue is a letter written to her infant son. The audience is, in this case, not at all the direct focus. And so on. Each of the monologues has an implied audience that may or may not be the same as the people sitting in the seats out front. And yet, though it may be focused imaginatively on a different audience, it still has to somehow include the people sitting in the seats out front.

• Other questions for each actress with a monologue to answer are: When is this taking place? And in what tense? In other words, am I speaking from a present tense, looking back on something that happened a short or long time ago, or even looking ahead to a future time? Jane Addams is speaking in 1915, in the present tense. Mildred Scott Olmsted and Toyomi Hashimoto are both speaking of the World War II era, but from a vantage point sometime beyond that. Congresswoman Barbara Lee and Amber Amundson both speak from the weeks and months immediately following the terrorist attacks of September 11 on the World Trade Center. The singers of "Ashes and Smoke" are looking to the future, affirming their intention to transmute tragedy into compassion and hope.

• A third important set of questions each actress should be able to answer about her monologue is: Why are you telling this? What do you want to have happen as a result of telling this? The stronger the verb that answers this question, the stronger the performance is likely to be. For example, if I am saying the words of a monologue in order to "tell" someone something, that's not going to be as strong a choice as if I'm saying those words in order to "inspire" or "challenge" or "comfort" or "spur to action," and the like.

Finding the Beats. In any monologue, and especially in the longer monologues, it's important to look for what actors and directors often call "the beats." These are places where something shifts or changes within the monologue. The clearer the actor is about when these times occur, the clearer will be the delivery of the words. A good example of how a piece has several changes of beat is Helen Caldicott's monologue. The piece moves through several different moods or shifts in attitude, culminating in a sequence that goes from gentle and serious to conspiratorial and humorous to deadly serious and challenging. The lines about how she felt so protective of her first baby's life are very gentle and serious, but they lead right into the wonderfully funny suggestion, which addresses the audience as co-conspirators, to flood the Senate chambers with naked toddlers. Just as her audience is laughing and delighting over that image, Caldicott turns blunt, "We're on a terminally ill planet, you know that, and we are about to destroy ourselves...." And then she issues the challenge: "You will realize you're going to have to change the priorities of your life—if you love this planet."

It's important to take time with each beat before shifting to the mood of the next one. Let the audience appreciate the gentle ferocity of the protective mother. Let them savor the idea of bringing naked toddlers to the Senate. Let them visualize the wisteria, the roses, all the things we cherish about the earth. Let them absorb the immensity of the challenge.

Another long monologue with many beats is Pamella Saffer's factfinding in Iraq. First is a title, terse almost: The Tigris and Euphrates. Seven thousand years of survival in the dessert. Then a confession of anguish, grief, and rage. Then the haunting memory of the very real people she's seen. Then indignation, given the facts and figures of the intensity of bombing. Finally, the resolve of the Iraqi families to survive is paralleled by the resolve of the speaker to keep fighting the good fight. No matter what the monologue (or dialogue), and no matter what its length, the actress should look for the beats within it. Playing a general attitude throughout a speech is a sure way to undercut its emotional power and clarity.

Let the Words Do the Work. How do we do this? It's a combination of letting the words affect us without planning in advance for what we think that effect should be, and careful analysis of the structure of the monologue looking for the clues that something is a moment of change in the internal life of the character. Take the "Ten Commandments on Vietnam," for example. Each of the lines of this piece refers to a different attitude or idea that was prevalent in at least some circles during the war in Vietnam. So it is important to let each of those ideas be clear in the actor's mind before the response refuting it is voiced. These are small shifts within the litany of the first nine commandments on Vietnam. There is a larger shift before the tenth commandment, because it is operating on several levels at once. First, it refers, as do the preceding nine, to the situation in Vietnam. But it also takes a step back from the specifics of the Vietnam War to the general ethical rule. Unbounded by time and space, it voices the commitment to nonviolence in all human affairs, everywhere, at all times. And finally, it operates on a deeply personal level, becoming the statement of both Dr. King and his grieving widow, who is only 24 days away from Dr. King's assassination and has put aside her personal grief to carry on the work of her slain husband. So that last line should never be rushed. There should be a beat of time just before it is delivered, which helps the audience to recognize that a shift is coming, and that something even more important is about to be said.

Another example, from the same section of the play, is the FBI memos. Though the content of these memos is actually chilling in that they reveal a mind-set that echoes the play's title to the effect that women who suggest peace might be preferable to war are dangerous and must be monitored closely, the pieces are also needed comic relief. The agents are so caught up in their roles that they don't see the absurdity of it, which is the essence of clown. Again, it is important to approach each monologue line by line, rather than taking a general attitude and playing it straight through, to get maximum effect. Agent 1's first line sets up the general character of the agent and the task the agent is fulfilling: writing a memo to the file about a particular demonstration. But another thing is happening in that line (or can be happening). That is the agent's attitude toward WILPF. We can presume—from an entire history of these women being considered dangerous and radical— that this agent might share a low opinion, and this can show in the voice. (By way of contrast, think of how the agent's voice might sound if he or she were reporting on surveillance of the President of the United States and felt that the president was the most important and wonderful leader of the century.) Again, given the history of mistrust and contempt for women who are activists, there's probably a little attitude that can show through on the use of the term "female." It depersonalizes the subject, creates an "us and them" mood. Then there are specific bits of evidence offered: Here's why these women are dangerous, they distribute handbills! But wait, there's more! These handbills actually contain information that tells how our taxpayers' moneys are spent!

At the end of each monologue comes a shift—the "I'm doing my job as an agent" tag line, letting anyone who reads the memo know that the appropriate other agencies have been notified of these scandalous events.

In a full staging, the agents should decide who the audience represents. If the audience is fellow agents, that will influence the monologues in one direction. If the audience is WILPF members, that will influence the monologues in a very different direction. In our productions to date, we've generally gone with the latter, aligning the audience with the women of WILPF and the agents with each other. (In one performance, we had great fun glaring at the real Marii Hasagawa, who was in the audience that night!) But the life of a play comes from investigating what works best for a given cast and audience, so it's useful to play around with different possibilities before settling on a specific staging and interpretation.

Throughout the more serious monologues, it is crucial for the performers to let the words affect them honestly rather than to try to push a highly emotional rendering. If the actors express all the emotion contained in the speeches themselves, there isn't much room for the audience to discover its own feeling. Though it may seem counterintuitive, a monologue will be much more moving to an audience when the actress who delivers it contains her powerful emotions rather than letting them all "hang out." There are some exceptions to this. Rosika Schwimmer is defined as a person who lets it all hang out, so when she comes out with the line, "We must thunder forth a demand for stopping this war in such a voice as will drown the canon's roar," the more thunderous and outspoken she can be, the better. But when Toyomi Hashimoto tells of the horrors of the Nagasaki bombing, the audience needs some space in which to absorb the words. Toyomi is composed, dignified, looking back on the event. How do I decide this? I look at the text. The final line to me is a tipoff. "Still he bore everything bravely and only asked, 'Am I being a good boy?'" Here is a cultural attitude summed up in one wrenching line. And if Toyomi's little boy is so clearly concerned with being a good, brave boy, we can surmise that his parents would behave similarly. I also get a clue from the source. The material was gathered in an oral history project, so I surmise that she might be speaking to a group of students who are studying their own country's history. This suggests to me that there might be an element of teaching in her monologue: making sure that the students understand what happened and understand how one comports oneself with dignity, courage, and compassion in the face of such extreme tragedy.

As you discover these nuances in the rehearsal process, think of the ways that even a small amount of movement can enhance and underscore the textual analysis. In long monologues, this could take the form of beginning the monologue at the seat, then moving downstage, or crossing stage right or left, before or during a second major beat in the monologue, and making one more move if there is another major beat in the piece. In Amber Amundson's open letter to President Bush, for example, she might take a brief pause, and a step further downstage, before delivering the summary of the speech, "So, Mr. President, when you say that vengeance is needed. . . . "

The narrative lines, too, should have such clarity of thought and energy behind them. The narrators, both the named narrators in Act I and all those who have narrative lines in either Act I or Act II, are usually speaking directly to the actual audience, that is, whoever is assembled to see the play at a given performance. But once in a while, they step in to the moment with another character or characters, as in the exchange with Jeannette Rankin in Act I or at the 4th International Congress.

In short, every line is there for a reason, so there are no "throwaway" lines. The narration is important because it gives the audience historical data and context; the character lines are crucial because they bring the history to life, connecting the narrative lines to flesh and blood folk.

Once you have worked with each actor so she knows exactly whom she is talking to, what the nuances are within her monologue or narrative responsibilities, and where the "beats" are, the next concern is to be sure that the audience will be able to hear all that glorious work.

Speak up! If you are performing the play for a large audience, in an auditorium or theater setting, you will—unless you have a cast that is fully trained and professional or unless you have a state of the art system of microphones and speakers—need to devote some time and attention to the art of projection. It's important to begin this early in the process for novice performers, because it takes some time to get used to how loud one sounds to oneself when one is sufficiently loud to be heard by a person in the back row of the theater. Here are a few tips and exercises you can share with your cast.

- **Diaphragmatic breathing** The easiest way to help people feel what this means is to ask each to place a hand over her belly, then practice breathing in a way that begins by pushing against that hand, opening up all the airways from the deepest possible place in the body. Keep the shoulders relaxed to avoid confusing puffing up the chest with actual deep breathing. On the exhalation, be sure to expel all the breath, down to the last vestiges. Breathing this way increases support for the voice so that it's possible to project without straining the throat muscles.

- **Warming up the throat** Starting with deep, diaphragmatic breathing, allow the breathing to be audible. Begin to make a humming sound, deep in the throat. Let that sound grow gradually louder with each exhalation. Feel the vibration from the humming relax the throat muscles. Finally, open the lips and make the sound an open-throated drone. Again, feel the vibrations relaxing the throat. Keeping the throat muscles relaxed, play around with the sound. Raise and lower the pitch. Change the shape of the mouth.

- **Focusing the sound**   Produce a droning sound as above. Imagine that you are directing the sound to the end of your nose. The tips of your toes. The person nearest you. The person across the circle from you. A person in the next room. A person in the next door building or outside. Bring it back inside the room, to the person near you, to your toes, to your nose. Repeat with words (say "hello" or say words from the play).

- **Talk to the wall**   After warming up the voice, practice loud declaration of lines neutrally to a spot on the wall. Practice often enough that you get used to hearing how loud you sound to yourself when you are sufficiently loud to be heard by others.

Practice in the Performance Space. Have someone sit in the back row and call "louder" if your voice isn't easily heard. Remember to keep your throat relaxed, support your voice, and focus your lines on that person sitting in the farthest seat from the stage.

Actors ask themselves a number of questions in order to effectively interpret their material:

Who am I (the character)?

Why am I telling this?

Who am I telling it to?

When am I telling it? (As it happens? Looking back on it?)

How am I telling it? (Writing a dispatch or letter? Speaking directly to an audience? Reading from a letter or essay? Composing an e-mail? Talking to a reporter?)

In what historical era am I telling it?

What do I hope to do by telling it?

Music Rehearsal. It is important to begin every music rehearsal with vocal warm-ups. Typically, a music director will lead the singers in a series of exercises that relax the throat, explore the vocal range, and practice articulation and resonance. Even if you are not an experienced music director, you can help your cast warm up by leading (or having someone in the cast who is musically inclined lead) some singing of scales and arpeggios, and some vocalizations up and down the scale using syllables ma, ta, na, za, and so on. With each syllable, notice where the sound vibrates in the body. Another simple warm-up is to make a sighing sound from the highest comfortable pitch to the lowest.

Several of the songs in *Most Dangerous Women* are fairly simple, musically speaking, and some are more complex. Some are somewhat well-known, or at least available on CDs and tapes to listen to, whereas others are original compositions that have yet to be professionally recorded. If you are producing *Most Dangerous Women* as a staged reading for an audience, see the Appendix F section to find out how to obtain sheet music and permission to perform the musical works in the show.

Some of the songs involve close harmonies ("As a Woman," "Ashes and Smoke," "Ja Sam Tvoj Svedok"). It's important to rehearse these early and often so that the somewhat unfamiliar intervals will become familiar. There's nothing quite so painful to the ear as a close harmony that isn't quite where it's supposed to be.

Each song functions within the play in a specific way. "Johnny I Hardly Knew Ya'" introduces the overall theme: the vow to stop war ("No they'll never take our sons again, Johnny I'm swearing to ya") with a song that pre-dates the First World War. "I Didn't Raise My Son to Be a Soldier" picks up this same theme, expressing the grief and frustration—of the mothers who attended the First International Congress and of mothers throughout the centuries. "There's a Way" serves to lighten the mood, reiterate some of the historical material, and introduce some new material, specifically, Jeannette M. Rankin's vote against our entry into that war. The reprise provides another bit of historical content, that WILPF members were among the first and few to speak out against the internment of Japanese Americans.

"Die Gedanken Sind Frei" is a song of resistance, needed to keep spirits up in the face of the Nazi juggernaut. "I Come and Stand at Every Door" haunts us with the voice and image of a child killed in Hiroshima. The singer asks for our commitment to the children of the world, who are the most innocent of all innocent victims of war. Again, there has been a promise made—as the narrator notes—that it shall not happen again.

As you rehearse the music, keep in mind the placement and mood of each song. Why is it needed at that particular point in the text? Is it to grieve? Provide comic relief? Inform? Stand up to power?

The songs in Act II are similarly specific in their placement and purpose. "If Every Woman" expresses the irrepressible hope of peacemakers. As Emily Greene Balch has noted, we must fill ourselves with the fresh air of courage and confidence. Karen MacKay's song is a song of courage and confidence. If we can envision it, we can work for it, even achieve it.

"Spell Against Sorrow" is another grieving song, expressing all the sorrow that came from the wars of the sixties, the assassinations, the loss of peaceful leaders like Dr. King. "As a Woman" picks up on something Jane

Addams talks about in Act I: that the women of WILPF see themselves first as citizens of the world, engaged in a common effort. "As a woman, the whole world is my country," the paraphrase of Virginia Woolf's famous line "As a woman, my country is the whole world," sums up this vision.

"Siph' amandla N'kosi" is a song that comes from the South African tradition of music inextricably bound up with protest and street action. Hundreds, probably thousands of songs were composed by the people of South Africa to keep their spirits intact during the long years of protest against apartheid. Like "Die Gedanken Sind Frei," it is a song of resistance to a power structure that imposes terror and inequity.

"No More Genocide," Holly Near's fierce song, speaks to the anger we in a democracy feel when we see our government making choices for war and destruction that we cannot support. "Ja Sam Tvoj Svedok" speaks to the powerlessness we feel when it seems all we can do is watch from the sidelines while evils unfold. At least we can bear witness. At least we can acknowledge what is happening.

"Children of Abraham" admonishes the parties in the Israeli-Palestinian conflict to look to their commonalities; the lyrics echo the sentiment in "As a Woman," in turn echoing the sentiment at the First International Congress, where there were no conspicuous flags. "Take down the flags that just separate the people," Arlo Guthrie wrote in his song, and that is what the women of the international women's peace movement constantly seek to do; what they did, in fact, do beginning with their First International Congress.

"Ashes and Smoke" is a hymm of our collective shock and grief over the attacks on the World Trade Center and Pentagon, and our determination to heal and grow stronger in this crucible.

"Singing for Our Lives" has become a sort of unofficial anthem of the Women's International League for Peace and Freedom, so it is a fitting finale to the show. It manages to say so much with so few words. We are gentle, yes. But we are not docile. We are angry. We are fueled by the knowledge that our very lives are at stake. And we are united across all boundaries, in spite of all flags, no matter where we are from, what language we speak, what our age, gender, sexual orientation, skin color. . . . And this is what makes us dangerous. We've made a promise to our sons, and to all the children of the world, and we mean to keep it.

So you see the music describes a kind of emotional arc of the play, punctuating, providing respite, expressing the strong emotions so contained in the monologue material. It isn't just a series of songs. There's a unity to it. The more the actresses can be aware of this unity and express it, the more compelling will the production be.

Putting It All Together. Even in a simple staging, where the actors are either seated in a semicircle or standing, there are a number of technical details to which actors should attend. The first is posture. It's important to sit straight and tall, both to provide adequate lung support to the voice and to create a stage picture of alertness, attention, and respect. Legs should be together, or crossed at the ankles, or with one foot slightly in front of the other. This detail helps to convey the historical sense of the play, too, as women during most of the twentieth century would have sat this way.

Scripts should be held slightly away from the body, supported with the left hand so the right is free to turn pages, and lower than facial level. Some novice performers have a tendency to hide behind the script, or to leave the script in their laps, which means they are looking down and unable to make eye contact with their audience.

As silly as it may sound, it may be useful to have a bit of page-turning rehearsal. Pages should be turned quietly, and basically at the same time. Actors can unwittingly upstage their colleagues by rustling their pages or turning them earlier than necessary. As magicians know, the audience's eyes follow movement, so movement that is unnecessary or premature will call attention to itself at the expense of whatever the audience is supposed to be paying attention to.

Speaking of scripts, it's important for the actors to keep their place. Encourage the performers to highlight their lines or otherwise mark them in a way that makes them easy to find quickly. Some visual learners may find it useful to highlight their cues as well, using a different color, for example, blue for cue lines (the phrase said just before an actor's line), and pink or yellow for their own lines. One trick is to mark an upcoming line with your right thumb while you listen to the lines prior so you can focus your attention on the person speaking and then quickly locate your own place in the script when it is time to do so.

The overall stage picture also deserves some attention. The suggestion in the script is for a basic semicircle shape (see Figure 4.1, page 122). In Act I the chairs or stools are clustered a bit within the overall arc, and in Act II there is more of a smooth rainbow curve to the shape. The key ingredients from a staging point of view are balance and visibility. Each actor should be able to see every other actor, and every audience member should be able to see every cast member. It may seem obvious, but it can take some planning to make sure this happens. If the music is performed with live musicians on stage, they need to be where the singers can hear them well.

Stage picture can be enhanced by some color coordination. If the scripts are in binders, they will look best if they are all the same neutral color:

black, gray, or beige. Glaring white should be avoided, as it can reflect light and become a visual distraction. Clothing colors should be coordinated so that there aren't visually distracting clashes of color.

The details of where actors are placed in the seating chart are important to work out ahead of time. This is the director's job. Placement of actors depends a great deal upon line assignments, music assignments, and overall cast size. Using small circles of paper with performers' names written on them on a scaled map of the stage is one way to facilitate this planning. When I am working on a production, I assign the first act narrator and large character monologues first, then look to balancing out with songs and shorter character monologues. Only after I feel that everyone is being heard in roughly equal measure do I begin to make the seating chart. The sample chart included in Figure 4.1 is for a cast size of 12 in Act I and 13 in Act II (because the young singer who appears at the end of Act I joins the cast in Act II).

Single narrative lines or words, for example, headline sequences, should be assigned once all the roles are set and the seating chart is determined. This enables you to assign quickly moving sequences of lines in predictable patterns, moving up and down the row of actors. Audiences will find it hard to follow the meaning of the words if they have to keep searching for which direction each one came from.

Movement. The script suggests some simple movement. A general principle is to stand on character monologues and remain seated on shorter narrative lines. Within longer monologues, actors can look for variety in how to approach this. For example, an actress might begin a monologue from her seat, then find a line on which to stand and move a bit. The director's job is to watch the overall picture, to make sure there isn't the effect of a mechanical, invariable approach to each monologue.

Whenever possible, the director should help the actors find reasons to relate to one another. Small examples suggested in the stage directions are reactions to lines such as the one describing Rosika Schwimmer's somewhat scandalous dress and behavior patterns or the headline declaring the first year of Prohibition a success. Larger opportunities come with segments such as the FBI memos, where the two actresses can engage with one another as fellow undercover agents or the poem "The Situation in Soweto Is Not Abnormal," in which the two speakers portray a chilling sort of over the back fence or neighborhood bar gossip about the brutality of enforcing the apartheid system. Other times when brief connections can be established through eye contact or physical contact are those points in the script where an actress has expressed strong emotion through a song or monologue. An affirming nod, a brief touch of a hand, these sorts of gestures help to create the feeling of ensemble on the stage and show to the audience that sense of solidarity that is described in so many of the narrative lines.

Pacing Details. The headline sections and the poem at the beginning of Act II "I Am a Dangerous Woman" generally need some specific pacing rehearsal. Especially in Act I, the headlines need to move briskly, ever more so as the pace of events leading up to war quickens and the outcome of war becomes harder to avoid. At the beginning of Act II, synchronizing the lines to the pace at which actresses come back to the stage takes a little extra attention so that there are no dead spaces between the stanzas of the poem and when each actress begins her stanza as she reaches the stage.

Technical Rehearsal. There is nothing quite like a tech rehearsal for tedium—unless you are part of the technical crew given a precious hour or two to do the several dozens of things on your list: focus lights, set light levels, set sound levels, set timing on cues, run the cues, fix the cues that didn't work right, run them again, and be ready to run the show flawlessly.

There are a few things you can do to facilitate tech rehearsals and make them relatively stress-free. First, especially if you are working with inexperienced actors, be sure to emphasize with your cast that the tech rehearsal is precisely that. It is not the time to be figuring out how to approach a monologue or polish a song. Help them understand that the show should be ready to go before the tech rehearsal.

Next, go through the script and be very clear about what you want technically. There are a few sound cues indicated, and a very few light cues. The only complicated cues are at the end of Act I, where the lights and sound must be coordinated with each other and precisely timed not only for effect, but to allow the actresses to leave the stage and return in the second blackout.

You may, if you have the expertise and the resources available, want to do something more complicated with the lighting design. You may, if you have no technical resources, simply be stationing someone by a light switch on the wall. In either case, try to work through all the cues with whomever will be running them in what is called a dry tech, which is to say, before the actors are present. A lot of questions can get asked and answered in a dry tech, which minimizes the time you need the cast to be there.

Once you've met with your tech crew and all the cues have been worked through in a dry tech, it's time to bring the actors on and run a cue to cue rehearsal. This is one in which only the material that is necessary to set up cues is run. The beginning of Act I, the sound cues in Act I, the end of Act I (the air raid cue and the very final moment), the beginning of Act II, and the end of the show are the essential cues to run, if you are doing the ones suggested in the script. Usually, your stage manager will call the cues, which starts with telling the sound and lighting technician(s) the lighting and sound (if any) to have on while the audience is taking its seats, then telling the actors to take their places offstage, ready to begin the show. Next, the stage manager will call the cue to take the house lights and stage lights out to the blackout level that begins the show, and tell the sound person to start the first sound cue, the sound of artillery fire. As that sound cue begins, the musicians and actresses who are performing "Johnny I Hardly Knew Ya'" have to take their places quickly and quietly in the dark. This might prove to be difficult, and you may have to start over at the beginning of the sequence and practice it a time or three before it happens without problems. There may be slight adjustments to the light levels, to provide just a whisper of light (called "ghost light"), or other strategies worked out for how the actresses find exactly where they should be on stage in the dark. Once all these details are polished and you've made it through the light cue that brings the lights up to their full level, you jump ahead to the very end of the song. Now it is time to rehearse the pacing of getting the rest of the cast on stage while each member says a line. Again, you may need to back it up, get them offstage, and start again at the first narrative line in order to run it more than once until there are no glitches, unnecessary pauses, stumbles, or other less than perfect moments.

So you proceed through the play, running only those sections that include either sound cues, light cues, major movement, or all three.

The tech rehearsal is the time, too, to set how you will do the curtain call. In some productions, the house lights have come up during the final song to encourage the audience to join in, and the actors leave the stage into/through the audience at the very end of the show. In other productions, the actors leave by the stage entrances/exits, and the house lights don't come up until they are offstage. These are tiny details, but if you've not done a show before, you'll be surprised at how time consuming they can be if you don't plan well for them. And you'll be chagrinned to find out how—if you don't polish that final moment—it can leave an impression of messiness and disorganization as the final image of all you've worked so hard to present well.

Fianl Rehearsal. Now you're ready for your final rehearsal, a full dress and tech. With luck, this is in your schedule. But it may be that the first time you actually have a chance to run through the entire piece with lights and sound is in front of your audience. That's why all the earlier rehearsal on individual parts, on pacing, and on cues is so important. Unless there is an unmitigated disaster during your final dress rehearsal, do not stop the show. During the earlier rehearsal process some actresses may get into the habit of correcting errors in reading, or may ask to begin a monologue over if they stumble or don't feel they've done it particularly well. This is your last chance to break that habit and instead practice pulling the show off with confidence, poise, and energy no matter what happens. Audience members don't see mistakes in the performance as much as they see the performance of mistakes. The actress who says "oops!" either literally or figuratively calls attention to the error. The actress who keeps the show going, never letting on that there has been an oops, will find that she is the only one who even noticed the glitch.

Talk Backs. You may want to schedule a talk back after your performance. This is an opportunity for those in the audience who are interested to come back or stay in their seats to participate in a discussion and question/answer session with the cast and crew.

2

Connecting to Themes in U.S. and World History

One of the benefits of taking the time to do a project such as *Most Dangerous Women* in the classroom is that it can become a touchstone and a springboard for the entire semester or year. A documentary distills a great deal of information into a relatively short period of time (two hours to cover over 90 years, for example!) and so any one line or speech in it can be unpacked, so to speak, into an extended inquiry. Whether you simply recall a line or section of the play as you teach the topics they relate to or stop to allow for in-depth research projects, the more connections you can help the students make between the text of the play and their history texts, the more memorable and meaningful will be their learning.

The following are several topics for discussion and extended research based in the script. They are not meant to represent the definitive or exhaustive list of such possible questions and research topics. Rather, they are offered here as examples of the many questions that can be generated from virtually any line in the script. In classrooms where *Most Dangerous Women* is read as part of a world history or United States history course, the script can provide touchstones throughout a semester or year that can be connected to the ongoing course content. Some of them could be very emotionally challenging for high school age students (as indeed they would be for adults), some of them less so. You would want to choose topics that were matched appropriately to your students' levels of emotional maturity as well as their levels of research skills.

Examining Song Lyrics

According to several sources, the opening song, "Johnny I Hardly Knew Ya'," dates originally from the early 1800s. Irish troops were heavily recruited by

England to serve in Ceylon (now Sri Lanka). Many came back with devastating injuries, as the song documents. During the American Civil War, the song was reframed as a celebratory one, "When Johnny Comes Marching Home." Compare the lyrics to any version of "Johnny I Hardly Knew Ya'" to those of "When Johnny Comes Marching Home." To whom does the song seem to be addressed in each case? Who seems to be the singer of the song in each case? What does the singer in each case think of war? What is the evidence from the song lyrics to support this? (See Appendix E for a worksheet of guiding questions.)

Research Questions. Find the full lyrics to "I Didn't Raise my Boy to be a Soldier" and to "Over There." (Inserting a song title into any search engine will generally produce multiple links to the lyrics.) Compare and contrast as above. Find lyrics to contrasting songs from other war eras, and compare and contrast. Two interesting sets of lyrics to compare from World War II are Pete Seeger's "Dear Mr. President" and Vern Partlow's "Old Man Atom (Talking Atom Blues)." The first captures the eagerness with which most Americans wanted to "lick Mr. Hitler," the second is a sobering reflection from the end of the war years on the awesome power of atomic energy. The Vietnam era produced a great deal of music, three strong viewpoints can be explored through comparing and contrasting lyrics to "The Ballad of the Green Beret" by SSgt. Barry Sadler and Robin Moore, "I Feel Like I'm Fixin' to Die Rag" by Country Joe MacDonald, and "Sam Stone" by John Prine. Pete Seeger's "Waist Deep in the Big Muddy" provides an interesting contrast of Seeger's opinion of the Vietnam war to how he felt about World War II as expressed in "Dear Mr. President." Two sets of contrasting lyrics from the war in Iraq are "Iraq and Roll" by Clint Black & Hayden Nicholas and "Final Straw" by REM.

Language Arts Connections. Analyze the images, arguments, and structures used in pro-war songs, anti-war songs, and songs that articulate a vision of peace. Informed by that analysis, write song lyrics that express each of the following: opposition to a war, support for a war, a vision of inevitable conflict, a vision of peace.

The Casualties of War

Two of the World War I headlines mention casualty figures from battles and disease: "Russians Lose 500,000 at Passes" and "Disease Spreads All over Serbia: 25,000 to 30,000 Cases of Typhus." Much was made of the fact that American deaths in the war in Iraq were over 2,100 at the end of 2005; Iraqi casualties were reported to be in the tens of thousands. The SARS

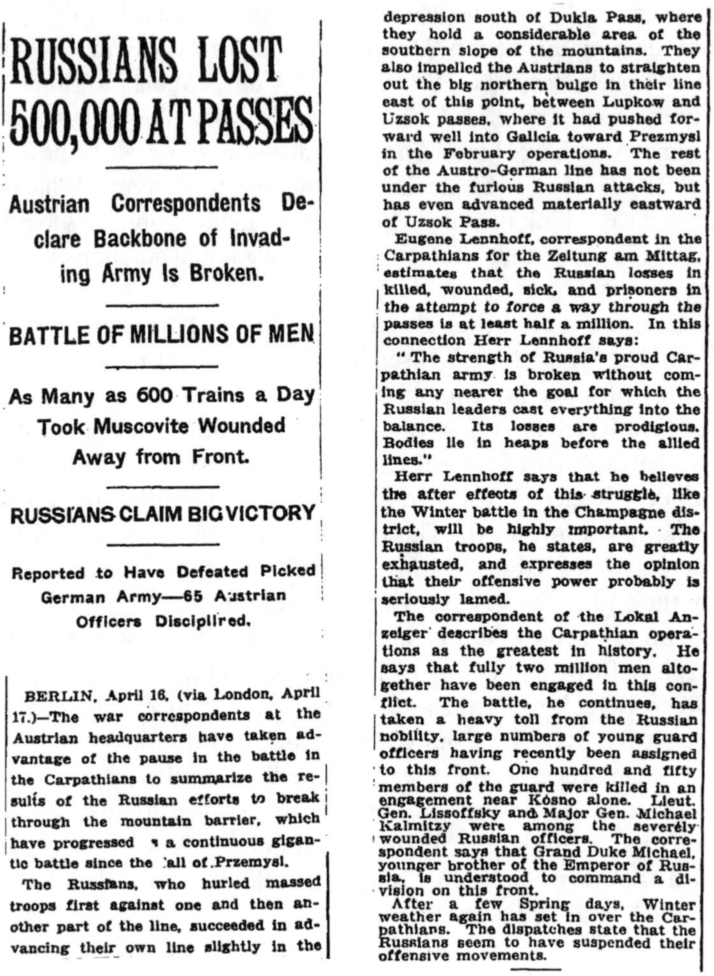

RUSSIANS LOST 500,000 AT PASSES

Austrian Correspondents Declare Backbone of Invading Army Is Broken.

BATTLE OF MILLIONS OF MEN

As Many as 600 Trains a Day Took Muscovite Wounded Away from Front.

RUSSIANS CLAIM BIG VICTORY

Reported to Have Defeated Picked German Army—65 Austrian Officers Disciplined.

BERLIN, April 16, (via London, April 17.)—The war correspondents at the Austrian headquarters have taken advantage of the pause in the battle in the Carpathians to summarize the results of the Russian efforts to break through the mountain barrier, which have progressed a continuous gigantic battle since the fall of Przemysl.

The Russians, who hurled massed troops first against one and then another part of the line, succeeded in advancing their own line slightly in the depression south of Dukla Pass, where they hold a considerable area of the southern slope of the mountains. They also impelled the Austrians to straighten out the big northern bulge in their line east of this point, between Lupkow and Uzsok passes, where it had pushed forward well into Galicia toward Prezmysl in the February operations. The rest of the Austro-German line has not been under the furious Russian attacks, but has even advanced materially eastward of Uzsok Pass.

Eugene Lennhoff, correspondent in the Carpathians for the Zeitung am Mittag, estimates that the Russian losses in killed, wounded, sick, and prisoners in the attempt to force a way through the passes is at least half a million. In this connection Herr Lennhoff says:

"The strength of Russia's proud Carpathian army is broken without coming any nearer the goal for which the Russian leaders cast everything into the balance. Its losses are prodigious. Bodies lie in heaps before the allied lines."

Herr Lennhoff says that he believes the after effects of this struggle, like the Winter battle in the Champagne district, will be highly important. The Russian troops, he states, are greatly exhausted, and expresses the opinion that their offensive power probably is seriously lamed.

The correspondent of the Lokal Anzeiger describes the Carpathian operations as the greatest in history. He says that fully two million men altogether have been engaged in this conflict. The battle, he continues, has taken a heavy toll from the Russian nobility, large numbers of young guard officers having recently been assigned to this front. One hundred and fifty members of the guard were killed in an engagement near Kosno alone. Lieut. Gen. Lissoffsky and Major Gen. Michael Kalmitzy were among the severely wounded Russian officers. The correspondent says that Grand Duke Michael, younger brother of the Emperor of Russia, is understood to command a division on this front.

After a few Spring days, Winter weather again has set in over the Carpathians. The dispatches state that the Russians seem to have suspended their offensive movements.

Figure 2–1. Caption: *War casualties in World War I were 10,000 times higher than today in Iraq.*

scare of 2003 involved a total of 251 deaths in eight countries, with 4,288 cases in 27 countries.

Discussion Questions. Why do you think we consider 2,100 to be a high number of American deaths when in previous wars the figures for our combat troops were much higher? Iraqi military and civilian casualties were considerably higher, but nowhere near the number of casualties sustained by the North Vietnamese, Viet Cong, and Vietnamese civilian population, nor the casualties sustained by any of the belligerent nations in World War II. Why are we so concerned about something that caused relatively few deaths, such as SARS, compared to the levels of fatalities from other diseases (such as AIDS and influenza) and other causes (such as traffic accidents)?

Research Questions. What are the total military and civilian casualties for each the following wars? Is there any trend evident? World War I, World War II, the war in Southeast Asia (1963–1975), the Gulf War, the war in Iraq, and the war on terrorism. (You may find that there are differing opinions as to when the war on terrorism actually began.) Which statistics are easiest to find? Are there different totals from different sources? How do you decide which is the most credible source/total?

Language Arts Connection. Read and discuss Dalton Trumbo's classic antiwar novel, *Johnny Got His Gun.*

Ancient Animosities

There is a headline (taken from the *New York Times,* as are most of the World War I headlines in the script) that says, "Kurds Massacre More Armenians." The dislocation and massacre of Armenians is a matter that to this day evokes strong emotions and fierce debate. Often, it is the Turks who are discussed as the instigators of the massacre, though they used Kurdish regiments in the Turkish army to carry out much of the campaign.

Discussion Questions. Genocides have occurred in all corners of the world, and the twentieth century saw more than any other to date: the Armenian massacre, the Jewish holocaust, the killing fields of Cambodia, "ethnic cleansing" in the former Yugoslavia, and the slaughter in Rwanda. On a lesser but still horrific scale were the tens, sometimes hundreds of thousands who lost their lives or liberty under repressive regimes in such places as Argentina, Iraq, and Uganda. What do you think makes people willing to participate in such horrific crimes against others? How do you think we can avoid these kinds of mass killings in the future?

Research Questions. What was the historical relationship between Turks, Kurds, and Armenians prior to the Armenian massacres? What were the reasons given by the Turkish government for its campaign against the Armenians in 1915? What has been the relationship among these three groups since then? What is the current status of the debate over how this event is referred to in historical accounts?

How were the countries of Iraq, Kuwait, and Syria, formed? Who drew the boundaries? When? What were the unresolved disagreements at that point historically? Have any of these issues been resolved, or are they still being contested today?

Literature Connection. Read and discuss any of the classical tragedies in which the tragedy is set in motion by ancient animosities or the thirst for revenge, for example, *The Oresteia, Romeo and Juliet, Titus Andronicus.*

Who Is "the World?"

Twelve countries were represented in the First International Congress of Women at The Hague.

Discussion Questions. Why were the participants from European and North American countries, but not other continents or countries? How does this compare to the number of countries represented in the Forum on Women that was part of the Beijing Conference in 1995? How does the number of member nations of the League of Nations compare to the number of member nations of the United Nations? Are there countries today that are not members of the United Nations?

Research Questions. Which of the countries represented at The Hague in the First International Congress were at war at the time and which were neutral? What were the issues from the point of view of each of the countries mentioned? What did each warring country want to achieve? Why did each warring country feel justified in being at war? What were the main arguments in the United States for going to war and against going to war? Which current member nations of the U.N are at war today, either with another nation or within their own national boundaries?

Language Arts Connections. Read and discuss Mark Twain's bitter satire "The War Prayer." Read and discuss Ly Le Haslip's memoir of growing up during the conflict in Vietnam and coming to the U.S. to live, *When Heaven and Earth Changed Places.*

Resolutions and Assumptions

Several resolutions came out of the first meeting at The Hague that included several statements or assumptions about war and alternatives to war. For example, there is an assumption stated that the masses of people do not want war and do not bring wars about. There is a position taken for dealing with international disputes through social, moral, and economic pressure.

Discussion Questions. Do you agree or disagree with the assumptions in the statements of resolution? Do you agree or disagree with the idea that international disputes should be dealt with through social, moral, and economic pressure rather than through armed conflict? Give evidence/rationale for your opinions.

Research Questions. To what degree were the recommendations in these resolutions achieved? How much did the League of Nations represent the goals of these resolutions? What institutions set up in the aftermath of World War I are still in existence today? How have these institutions been involved in conducting warfare or facilitating peace? What are the details of Representative John Murtha's plan for withdrawing U.S. troops from Iraq? What is the substantive debate on his plan?

Language Arts Connection. Write a set of resolutions to express the vision of a peaceful withdrawal of United States troops from any area of conflict in the world in which the United States is engaged.

Negotiation

The third verse of the song "There's a Way" refers to a remarkable event: "the women weren't just talkers, they set out to see all the heads of state, 'Negotiate' their simple plea." Small committees of women set out from the congress at The Hague to plead with prime ministers, presidents, foreign secretaries, ambassadors, and kings, both in countries already at war and in countries that were—at least for the time being—still neutral. They asked the belligerent nations to commit to negotiations and the neutral nations to commit to leading the way.

Discussion Questions. Do people today have the same access to government? Are they the same people who had access to government in 1915 or different? How do ordinary citizens gain access to elected government today?

Research Questions. What are the skills/approaches used by professional negotiators? Which NGOs support or consistently urge the same approach to conflict? Are there wars that didn't happen because negotiations successfully headed them off? What conditions allowed for negotiated settlements and how are/were they different from the conditions in which wars seem inevitable? Under what auspices did these negotiations occur? How long did they take?

Language Arts Connection. Apply the negotiating process to characters in fiction. If two characters are in mortal conflict of some kind, how might a skilled negotiator get them to realize their common interests in a peaceful resolution to their differences? How would such a negotiator work with Antigone and Creon, for example? The Montagues and the Capulets?

Blockades

"Food is a subject that has never left my mind since I got here," says Dr. Alice Hamilton in the aftermath of World War I. "The continuation of the Allied food blockade for months after the armistice seems almost a worse crime against humanity than the war itself."

Discussion Questions. Do you think food blockades are appropriate exercises of international power? For people who support food blockades, what is/ might be the reasoning behind them? What about blockades of medical supplies and equipment?

Research Questions. The United States maintained a food blockade against Cuba after 1963. How did it affect the Cuban economy? What was the U.S. rationale for blockading food and medical supplies to Cuba? Does the policy seem to have achieved its objective? What were the terms of the blockade against Iraq following the Gulf War? What were the effects? Find examples of other kinds of blockades in history, such as weapons blockades. Compare and contrast the purposes of the different kinds of blockades, how effective they seem to have been, and who has suffered the most from their effects.

Language Arts Connection. Write a letter to the editor either supporting or criticizing a blockade currently in effect. Give evidence/reasons for your position rooted in history.

Treaties and Terms

"Harsh terms of Allies may drive Germans to uprising," said a headline following World War I.

Discussion Questions. How should countries defeated in war be treated? Should they lose land? Be forced to pay reparations? Have their imports of food, medicine, and technology controlled? Be required to disarm? What kinds of peace terms do you think will lead to the most lasting peace? Does it make a difference if the defeated country is perceived as the aggressor? Why or why not?

Research Questions. Review the terms of the Versailles Treaty. What parts of it were offensive to the Germans? If you were part of the negotiating team, would you have proposed any changes in the Treaty? How was Hitler able to use the dissatisfaction of Germans to build his Nazi party movement? Are there any parallels to situations in the world today? Review the treaty with Japan that ended World War II. Compare and contrast treaty provisions and historical consequences with the Versailles Treaty.

Language Arts Connection. Write parallel interior monologues of the subjects that "don't leave a person's mind" for "persons on the street" who have been on opposing sides of a conflict, responding to the terms of various treaties and armistice agreements throughout history, such as the Treaty of Versailles, the treaty with Japan (at the end of World War II), the armistice that ended hostilities between Israel, Egypt, Syria, Jordan, and Lebanon in 1949.

Freedom of Thought

"Die Gedanken Sind Frei"—the German song of resistance—lyrics go back to the 1500s.

Discussion Questions Is there something about the power of free thinking that will always triumph over tyranny? Cite examples of how people have survived very stressful and life-threatening circumstances by having "free thoughts."

Research Questions. Find biographies and autobiographies of people who've been prisoners of war, falsely incarcerated, or otherwise kept in bondage for a long period of time. How did they maintain their sense of their thoughts being free, being their own? What sorts of things have oppressive governments and other institutions (whether rebel forces or legally in power forces) done to try to control the "free thoughts" of people under their power/influence? How have people resisted? (Possible subjects include Aung San Suu Kyi, Nelson Mandela, Senator John McCain, or journalist Terry Anderson.)

Language Arts Connections. View and discuss the film *The Manchurian Candidate.*

Civilian Casualties vs. Military Casualties

According to the City of Hiroshima, approximately 140,000 civilians were killed in Hiroshima (out of a total population of 300,000–400,000) by the end of 1945 as a direct result of the bombing. In Nagasaki, the deaths by year-end 1945 were approximately 70,000 (out of an estimated 250,000). By 1950, the number of deaths attributed to these bombings had grown to 340,000. Defenders of the bombings say that it brought the war to an end, saving the lives of soldiers and civilians that would have been lost had the war continued.

Discussion Questions. Do you think civilian casualties are justified if military lives are saved as a result? Are civilian casualties of an enemy country justified if they save lives of United States citizens? Is there an acceptable ratio of lives for lives, for instance, is it worth more than one enemy life to save a life of a U.S. citizen?

Research Questions. Find out how many lives are estimated to have been saved by the bombings of Hiroshima and Nagasaki. What was the rationale behind choosing Hiroshima as a target? Why the second bomb on Nagasaki? There are some who point to a mistranslation of the Japanese response to the U.S. ultimatum, saying the Japanese sent a "no comment pending decision" message that was mistranslated as "we are ignoring your ultimatum." Find out what you can about this. Would it have changed the decision of Truman if the translation had been accurate? The atom bomb was developed based on scientific theories that were originally put forth by Albert Einstein. Find out what role Einstein played in the development of the atom bomb and what he felt about its use on Japanese cities.

Language Arts Connection. Read and discuss John Hersey's *Hiroshima*, Kyoko and Mark Selden's *The Atomic Bomb: Voices from Hiroshima and Nagasaki,* and/or other survivors' accounts. Write parallel editorial opinion essays about the bombings of Hiroshima and Nagasaki from the 1945 points of view of a Japanese citizen, a nuclear physicist, an American serviceman fighting in the Pacific, and/or any other roles you feel can shed light on some aspect of the decision.

Keeping Hope Alive

"Human nature seems to me like the Alps," Emily Greene Balch said. "The depths are profound and terrifying but the heights are equally real."

Discussion Question. What are some of the heights of human experience/ best aspects of human nature that can be seen in what we know of history and of current events?

Research Questions. Many countries and peoples have experienced horrific times in their history. How have they gone about trying to heal the wounds?

Some countries and groups to research include South African natives victimized by the apartheid system, Chilean victims of the Pinochet regime, Cambodian victims of the Khmer Rouge, Rwandan victims of genocide, the Jewish, Gypsy, trade unionist, political activist, and homosexual victims of Nazi extermination efforts, Native Americans, and African Americans. Are there commonalities in how peoples approach the healing process on such a large scale? Differences? Do any of the choices seem to be better than others? Which Nobel Peace Prizes have been awarded to those working in this arena for peaceful conflict resolution?

Language Arts Connections. Collect quotations on hope, and post them around the room. Write a letter to a personal friend or a journal entry about how you get through difficult times. Read selections from *The Impossible Will Take a Little While.*

Just and Unjust Wars and Conflicts

Some who were opposed to most wars put aside their pacifism to support the war against Hitler and Naziism (Mary Sheepshanks, for example). Others did not (Jeannette Rankin, for example).

Discussion Questions. Are there ways to control an aggressor short of war? What are the risks? What are the possible benefits?

Research Questions. How did the Danish citizenry resist Naziism? How did India win independence? How was apartheid ended in South Africa? What was the Velvet Revolution? What did it accomplish? What was the Orange Revolution?

Language Arts Connection. Write a persuasive essay that argues for or against the idea that wars can be just wars.

Postwar Repression

World War I was followed by a period of repression in the U.S.; World War II was followed by the Cold War and McCarthyism. In the aftermath of September 11, there have been similar responses.

Discussion Questions. Why would repression be a response to war? How should we balance our commitment to civil liberties with our desire for security?

Research Questions. Find out what legislation, if any, was passed after World War I that affected civil liberties. Similarly, find out if there was such legislation passed after World War II. Compare and contrast what you find in the post World War I and World War II eras to the provisions of the Patriot Act passed after the September 11 attacks.

Language Arts Connection. Read and discuss *The Crucible*, by Arthur Miller.

Homelands

England took control of Palestine in 1923, under a League of Nations mandate.

Discussion Questions. By what right or assumption of rights was it justified for England to control this area? Who had controlled it before World War I? If the holocaust in Europe had not happened, would Israel have been created as a state? Does everyone deserve a homeland, no matter how long ago they were initially dispossessed? If so, should Americans of European descent go back to Europe? Should the Chinese leave Tibet? What are other examples of this nature?

Research Questions. What was the situation with regard to Jewish settlers and Palestinians prior to World War II? What are the roots of the claims made on both sides of the conflict to the territory they wish to control? Are there models for cooperation and peaceful coexistence in the area and/or in the history of the region? What role has the United States played in brokering a peace in the Middle East? What were the terms of the agreement brokered by Ralph Bunche in 1949 that ended the first war between the newly created Israel and its neighbors?

Language Arts Connections. Read Palestinian and Israeli poems of place, such as "I Come from There" by Mahmoud Darwish and "Jerusalem" by Yehuda Amichai. (For a broader focus, include other countries/cultures, such as "Flowers for My Homeland" by Wole Soyinka, "To Lord Hu" by Li Ch'ing Chao, "Kabul" by Mirza Muhammed Ali Saib.) Write homeland poems.

The Role of Print Media in Finding the Truth

The Gulf of Tonkin resolution launched full-scale U.S. involvement in Vietnam, yet it was later found to be highly questionable whether an attack actually had occurred. The sinking of the battleship Maine was our reason for going to war with Spain, though 75 years later it was determined that the ship sank because of a malfunction, not attack by Spanish forces. Our war in

Iraq was justified in order to find and destroy weapons of mass destruction, yet none have been found.

Discussion Questions. Is it important to keep from going to war on false grounds? Is it possible? If so, what would be the safeguards necessary? If not, what are the reasons we will always be vulnerable to starting wars on insufficient or false information?

Research Questions. Read newspaper accounts of the Maine incident, the Gulf of Tonkin incident, and the charges that Iraq had weapons of mass destruction prior to the 2003 U.S.-led invasion and editorial responses to these news items. Read newspaper accounts of the revelations of doubt about the Maine incident, the Gulf of Tonkin incident and the existence of weapons of mass destruction in Iraq and editorial responses to each of these revelations. Compare and contrast the varying accounts and editorial stances.

The Race against Our Own Worst Possibilities

H. G. Wells said, "Human history becomes more and more a race between education and catastrophe." And Helen Caldicott puts our situation in similarly stark terms: " We're on a terminally ill planet, you know that, and we are about to destroy ourselves. . . . You're going to have to change the priorities of your life—if you love this planet."

Discussion Questions. In what ways do we need to educate ourselves in order to avoid the catastrophe of nuclear war? What are all the things we need to know? Who should be responsible for making sure we know them? Is war the only way in which humans are endangering their own future?

Research Questions. How many nuclear weapons does the United States have? Who are the other nuclear powers in the world? How many nuclear weapons do they have? Is it reasonable to expect non-nuclear nations to remain so? What were the terms of the SALT treaties? The Comprehensive Test Ban Treaty? The Nuclear Non-Proliferation Treaty? What is the current status of those agreements? What is the scientific evidence of global warming? What might be the results? What has been the political response of various interest groups and governments to this issue?

Language Arts Connection. Write an op ed piece either supporting or opposing the United States signing a multination treaty agreeing to reduce nuclear stockpiles, or supporting or opposing the United States signing on to the Kyoto Protocol.

The Power of One

Jeannette M. Rankin stood with few others in her vote against our entry into World War I. By the time the Congress voted on our entry into World War II, she was the single vote against. Representative Barbara Lee cast the only vote against granting President George W. Bush war powers to retaliate against terrorists in any way he deemed appropriate.

Discussion Questions. Why didn't anyone else vote with Rankin and Lee? Would you be willing to be the single vote for or against something? To be one or one among a few to take a public stand that might subject you to ridicule or violence?

Research Questions. Find accounts of the student protests in Tiananmen Square in Beijing, China, in June 1989, and in particular of the lone man who halted tanks by standing in front of them. See what you can find out about this man, what moved him to take the action he did, and what became of him.

Language Arts Connections. Read biographies of people who have made a great deal of difference in the lives of others because they were willing to stand alone in public on an issue and hold to what they thought was right in spite of opposition. Some might have had support from minority communities, but were willing to be the public test cases for a movement. Others might have had a strong personal vision that eventually brought others to their cause. Figures to read about might include Joan of Arc, Ruby Bridges, Rosa Parks, Jeannette M. Rankin, Vaclav Havel, Noam Chomsky, Emma Goldman, Paul Robeson, Mother Jones . . . or anyone else who has taken an initially unpopular and/or obscure stand and stuck with it.

Flags

In Amber Amundson's open letter to President Bush, she says, "When we buried my husband, an American flag was laid over his casket. My children believe the American flag represents their dad. Please let that representation be one of love, peace, and forgiveness."

Discussion Questions. What does the American flag represent to you? What does it represent to people who fly it on the Fourth of July? What does it represent to people who protest by burning it? What does it represent to immigrants who come to this country? What does it represent to citizens of countries who are enemies of the United States?

Research Questions. What is represented on various the flags, including the flag of the United Nations and the Earth Flag? What has our Supreme Court in the United States said about the flag of the United States and what it represents?

Language Arts Connections. Write a story or poem from the point of view of a flag. Write an editorial or letter to the editor taking a stand for or against the proposed constitutional amendment to make burning or otherwise defacing the flag of the United States illegal.

Children in War, Children in Peace

Children are the most innocent of innocent victims of war. Not only are they apt to lose parents, siblings, and homes, have their schooling interrupted, and be malnourished; they are also often forced to fight as soldiers or serve as prostitutes. Children are also vulnerable to exploitation in the market place, sometimes living as virtual slaves of employers who take advantage of them. Children in countries that are enjoying peaceful conditions and economic prosperity are, by contrast, unbelievably lucky and privileged.

Discussion Question. What are some of the ways young people in our country can help other young people, whether orphaned by war (including those in the United States), exploited as child labor, or displaced by economic or civil upheaval?

Research Questions. Who are some young people who have formed large-scale organizations or efforts to alleviate the suffering of other young people in the world? (One such person is Craig Kielburger, founder of Free the Children.) How did they get involved? What are they doing. How can other young people in this country join or begin efforts in their own communities to support other young people who are the victims of wars, economic exploitation, and other forms of abuse?

Language Arts Connections. Write letters to existing organizations requesting information about what they do. Write editorials or letters to the editor suggesting policies that could help children around the world.

Guiding Questions that Connect to the National Council for the Social Studies Ten Strands

Teachers who are using the framework of the Ten Social Studies Strands developed by the National Council for the Social Studies may find the following questions useful to connect the issues in *Most Dangerous Women* to the Strands.

The NCSS Strands

Culture. What are examples of cultural issues that cause conflicts between people, peoples, and nations? How can understanding the cultural attitudes and practices of another nation's peoples help to resolve international disputes peacefully?

Time, Continuity, and Change. How have the settlements of wars either mitigated against renewed conflict or seeded the conditions that lead to more war? How have the ways in which wars are fought changed over the decades/centuries? How has the effect on civilian populations changed? What are examples of peace threading through the centuries?

People, Places, and Environments. How are natural boundaries important in defining nations? How does competition for natural resources and access to waterways play a role in international disputes?

Individual Development and Identity. How do people learn to be peaceful? To go to war? What influences us to resolve conflicts either peacefully or violently? Can people change? What influenced Jane Addams to be the way she was? What influenced Saddam Hussein to be the way he is?

Individuals, Groups, and Institutions. What institutions influence people with regard to military conflicts? How do religious institutions play a role in what people believe about peace and war? How do political action organizations operate? How do anti-war organizations operate?

Power, Authority, and Governance. What is the process by which war is declared in the United States? How did that change in the most recent war in Iraq? What does our Constitution have to say about issues of war and peace? When and how does the government have the authority to require military service?

Production, Distribution, and Consumption. How do resources influence nations to go to war or to negotiate peaceful treaties and alliances? What were the resource disputes involved in World War I? In World War II? In Vietnam? In the Gulf War? The war in Iraq? How is what we want different from what we need?

Science, Technology, and Society. How has technology affected the fighting of wars? How has it influenced the seeking of peace? (Think not just of weapons systems but also of technologies such as the Internet, which are being used to organize peace efforts.)

Global Connections. How has the atomic era made a global village of us all? How has the Internet had that same effect? What are issues in the world today that go beyond any one country's interests, needing to be addressed on a global scale?

Civic Ideals and Practices. What is the obligation of a citizen when there is a potential war? How does a citizen become adequately and accurately informed in order to decide what kind of position to take? What civic ideals and practices help lay the foundation for lasting peace?

3

—

Creating Original Readers' Theater Projects

Y ou may find that you would like to have other documentary Readers'
Theater texts for your students to work with. Perhaps you would like
them to take on the challenge of creating a documentary Readers'
Theater script. Or perhaps you feel inspired to take some time over the sum-
mer to create a script tailored to your specific classes and students. This
chapter outlines the pieces you may want to include and suggests some principles of overall structuring for optimum dramatic effect.

Basic Definitions

First, let's review some definitions. In its simplest form, Readers' Theater
means that the actors sit or stand with scripts in hand and read from the text
rather than staging actions and memorizing lines. In one variation of the
form, a narrative with essentially a single point of view is broken up among
several readers. The poem at the beginning of Act II of *Most Dangerous
Women* is a mini-example of this approach. Written by a single author (Joan
Cavanagh) with a single point of view, it is broken into seven sections, or
"voices." Other material that might be turned into Readers' Theater this way
could include famous speeches (e.g., Patrick Henry's "Give me liberty or give
me death" oration, or Martin Luther King Jr.'s "I have a dream" speech), long
poems (Mark Twain's "The War Prayer"; Maya Angelou's "On the Pulse of
Morning"), essays (George Orwell's "On Shooting an Elephant" or "Politics
and the English Language"), and short stories written in a narrative voice
without dialogue (Tim O'Brien's "The Things They Carried").

Another variation is a staged reading of a story or narrative in which
there is a narrator voice and one or more character voices. This structure is

well suited to exploring and dramatizing short stories in which there is a fair amount of dialogue as well as narrative material.

The focus of this book is what I call documentary Readers' Theater, that is to say, the kind of theater that has as its purpose the exploration of a particular issue from multiple points of view, with the aim of incorporating and condensing researched historical material. Though it may, and often does, include poems, songs, and other source material that is fictional in its structure, the main focus is on telling a story that is nonfiction.

A basic guide to creating this kind of Readers' Theater can be found in *History in the Present Tense: Engaging Students through Inquiry and Action*, Chapter 7, "Making History." There you will find a discussion of how high school students, guided by teachers and guest artists, researched and created documentary Readers' Theater plays in order to communicate learning about the World Trade Organization, the Japanese American experience from immigration through redress, and labor history.

What Are the Pieces?

Whether you research and create the text yourself or have your students create it through research and collaboration, the pieces are essentially the same.

Theme

Look for

- an issue of importance to your course of study. You're going to be spending some time with this, so you don't want the content to be tangential.
- a topic that will permit you to explore either several sides of a controversial issue or an aspect to an issue that is not otherwise included in the course materials.
- a topic that you know will allow you to consult a variety of source materials.
- corroboration of the "facts" you discover in your sources; alternatively, clear attribution of the source of opinions and the agendas of those sources.

Where Do You Get Ideas?

The index of your adopted textbook is a good place to start. I am looking at one widely used textbook for American history and seeing possibilities in virtually every chapter. It's a matter of asking those two questions: What topics are mentioned that are presented somewhat simplistically but are/were controversial, and what topics are scarcely mentioned at all but would contribute to a richer understanding of history? Some of the better texts may even include material on controversial issues from a couple of points of view but that is generally the limit. The various nuanced points of view of American colonists, for example, are generally boiled down into Tories and Revolutionaries, pro or against British rule. But these positions came from complex debates and interactions of forces every bit as difficult to sort out at the time as might be the positions of Iraqi citizens today, trying to figure out where to place their loyalties in a chaotic and unpredictable situation.

The Civil War is on every scope and sequence chart for American history. Most of the history text content is focused on the debates in Congress over free versus slave states and the battles of the Civil War. What are some of the histories hidden by this focus that might be explored through documentary theater? Contributions of and resistance of enslaved African people is one possibility. From the musical traditions of the spirituals, where Bible stories provided metaphors of escape and deliverance, to quiet and secret subversive acts such as learning to read, armed rebellions, clever and daring escapes, there is much to explore to help students understand that enslaved people were skilled and accomplished survivors.

Another topic in American history that affords rich opportunities for developing documentary Readers' Theater is the Great Depression. There are wonderful sources of firsthand accounts and still many survivors of those hard times who might love to share their memories with students or a teacher. Music from the era is readily accessible. Facts and figures are abundant. Essays, pieces of legislation, and newspaper accounts are all fairly easy to come by, and other documents such as foreclosure papers, eviction notices, personal journals and letters, and the like may also be waiting to be discovered in local, state, and national archives, or attics and basements of students' great-grandparents.

If you choose a topic that is more distantly in the past, you will be somewhat more limited in your resources; however, there are still plenty of points of view discoverable and plenty of documents to browse if you know where to look. One place to look is the Internet. You will find something on just about anything you care to search for. Of course, the source may or may not be credible. That's something you will have to either sort out yourself or teach your students how to assess, but Internet discoveries can help you formulate guiding questions to pursue with your local reference librarian. Also, Internet sites often mention published sources that you can request from your library. I know there is increasing concern about students who do all their research on the Internet, never learning how to browse an actual bookshelf in an actual library. The ease with which anything, no matter how outrageous or lacking in factual basis, can make its way into cyberspace is a definite concern. But nothing beats the Internet for up-to-the-minute leads. This is true even for events far in the past, as every day more and more resources are added to the Internet.

Timelines

Timelines are widely available on the Internet and in print for virtually any segment of human history or prehistory you may wish to investigate. Adhering to a chronological structure as your basic skeleton helps your readers or your audience, whether it is as contained as the students in your classroom or as open as the general public, to make sense of the events you are portraying. Timelines can show a gathering storm or the facets of a public debate as well. Many timelines are subject to copyright, so if you plan to use them word-for-word beyond your classroom, you will need to request permission from rights' holders. Alternatively, write your own descriptions for the events, based on the timeline as a reference.

Here's an example of timeline items that can convey the sense of growing economic crisis during the Great Depression. These items could stand together in a sequence (as the headlines leading up to World War I and World War II do in *Most Dangerous Women*) or could be interspersed with longer bits of narrative, other kinds of headlines, and/or music.

1929: U.S. Stock Market Collapses

1930: 1,350 banks suspend operations

1931: 4 to 5 million unemployed in the United States; another 2,293 banks suspend operations

1932: 1,493 more banks suspend operations

1933: 4,000 additional banks suspend operations

Below is a timeline constructed to convey the sense of public debate and discord during the Vietnam War era. I developed a first draft in about two hours, using the Internet as the primary research tool. My next step was to condense several pages of items. For purposes of the example here, I've limited the timeline to the first three years of the war, beginning with the Gulf of Tonkin resultion. (A truly thorough exploration could go back at least as far as the first U.S. military advisors arriving in Vietnam.)

A crucial next step in this process would be to fact-check all the figures (which I have not yet done). Dates and statistics on the Internet can vary widely from one source to another. It's important to find agreement among credible sources on such things as dates, estimated crowd sizes, numbers of military and civilian casualties, and troop levels. It's important, too, to track the source of direct quotations and make sure they are accurate.

First Draft: A Vietnam War Timeline 1964–1967

1964: U.S. Congress passes the Gulf of Tonkin Resolution, giving President Johnson the power to take whatever actions he sees necessary to defend southeast Asia.

1965: February: Johnson at 70 percent approval rating. Authorizes Rolling Thunder bombing offensive.

March: Johnson authorizes use of napalm and "search and destroy" missions.

April: Combat strength raised to more than 60,000 troops. First major anti-war march in Washington draws up to 25,000.

July: Johnson announces increase to 125,000 troops, doubles monthly draft calls to 35,000.

November: 35,000 anti-war protesters circle the White House, then rally at Washington Monument.

December: U.S. troop level reaches 184,300.

1966 January: Senator Robert F. Kennedy criticizes President Johnson's war policies.

February: The Senate Foreign Relations Committee holds televised hearings examining America's policy in Vietnam.

March: Anti-war protests are held in New York, Washington, Chicago, Philadelphia, Boston, and San Francisco.

July: U.S. bombs North Vietnamese troops in the Demilitarized Zone separating North and South Vietnam.

August: U.S. planes bomb South Vietnamese village by mistake: 63 civilians killed, over 100 wounded.

November: Defense Secretary McNamara is confronted by student protesters during a visit to Harvard University.

December: American forces in Vietnam reach 385,000; 60,000 more stationed offshore. 6,000 Americans have been killed in 1966; 30,000 wounded.

1967 January: Senator J. William Fulbright publishes *Arrogance of Power*, criticizing America's war policy and advocating peace talks between Viet Cong and South Vietnamese government. President

Johnson calls Fulbright, Robert Kennedy, and other critics in Congress "Nervous Nellies."

February: Nationwide "Fast for Peace" staged by American religious groups.

March: Congress authorizes $4.5 billion to fund war effort.

April: Richard M. Nixon charges anti-war protestors are prolonging the war; 200,000 attend demonstrations in New York and San Francisco. Rev. Martin Luther King Jr. says Johnson's social reform programs are undermined by the war.

May: The United States is condemned at a mock war crimes tribunal organized by Bertrand Russell in Stockholm.

August: California Governor Ronald Reagan says because "too many qualified targets have been put off limits to bombing," the United States should get out of Vietnam.

October: Forty-six percent of Americans now believe U.S. military involvement in Vietnam is a mistake, feel the United States should either win or get out. *Life* magazine retracts earlier support of Johnson's war policies. Fifty-five thousand protestors march on the Pentagon.

November: Defense Secretary Robert McNamara resigns, joining other top Johnson aides Bill Moyers, McGeorge Bundy, and George Ball who have resigned over the war. Democrat Eugene McCarthy announces he will oppose Johnson in primaries as an anti-war candidate.

December: During four days of anti-war protests in New York, baby doctor Benjamin Spock is among those arrested. Troop levels are at 463,000. Combat deaths to date are 16,000. Over 1 million soldiers have rotated through service in Vietnam.

Headlines

Structurally, headlines are very similar to timeline items, so their effect dramatically is somewhat similar. Because they are more closely focused on specific events, they give more the flavor of an era than an inclusive summary. Headlines are not subject to copyright, so they can be quoted freely in documentary texts. One of the best ways to locate headlines is to browse the microfiche newspaper collections at the local public or college library. A wonderful online resource is the New York Times website, which allows you to browse headlines as far back as 1851. You'll find a link on their homepage at http://www.nytimes.com. A search using the terms "Vietnam" and "protests," then another using "LBJ" and "Vietnam" yielded pages of headlines. The few I've listed below were selected to show the tension between opponents of U.S. involvement in Vietnam and both Johnson and Nixon as presidents:

August 1964: Johnson Calls Air Strike Warning to Aggressors

August 1965: 200 Parade in Time Square to Protest U.S. Role in Vietnamese War

October 1965: Johnson Decries Draft Protests

February 1967: Dance: Angry Arts at Hunter College

October 1967: Thousands Reach Capital to Protest Vietnam War

December 1967: Draft Violators Face Stiff Curbs

February 1968: 2,000 March Here to Protest War

October 1969: Nixon Vows Again Not to Be Swayed by War Protests

October 1969: How Moratorium Grew into Nationwide Protest

Brief Quotations

Snippets of comments, especially from historical contemporaries of the events and/or well-known figures, that sum up attitudes on various sides of an issue put human faces and feelings on the issues. In *Most Dangerous Women*, for example, in both the First International Congress and the section on the 1995 Beijing Women's Conference, quotes from both detractors and participants convey some of the controversy and human emotion that surrounded the events. Where do you find such quotations? Letters to the editor, in the body of news articles, in newspaper and other media editorials, in scholarly works about the topic or era, in oral history interviews with survivors of the era/events you are focusing on, and last but not least in quotation databases, both print published and on the Internet. I find it useful to keep a word processing file labeled "for possible use" or "quotations relevant to . . . ." or something of that nature where I can keep the excerpts and quotations until I am ready to assemble the text.

Longer Monologues

Longer monologues allow you to explore the deep impact of historical events on human lives. Look for them in scholarly works, memoirs, transcripts of oral histories, and anthologies that include essays and memoirs such as *The Impossible Will Take a Little While*, *My Country is the Whole World*, and *Women on War* (see Appendix F for further title information). You may find open letters that are posted from people directly affected by or witnessing current events;

editorial essays, online journals, and blogs (weblogs); and statements made by public figures—either on their websites or in media coverage. Examples of such monologues in *Most Dangerous Women* include Mildred Scott Olmsted's recollections of the Nazi era and the role she played in resistance, Amelia Boynton's memories of the civil rights struggle, Representative Barbara Lee's statement after the events of September 11, 2001, and Amber Amundson's open letter to President Bush.

Poems and Songs

Poems and songs can serve several purposes in a documentary. They give us a break to contemplate—a chance to digest/express emotionally what we are feeling at a particular point ("Spell Against Sorrow", "Ashes and Smoke"). They can give us related information, either reinforcing a key idea that has already been expressed (as in Verse 1 of "There's a Way") or adding details (as in Verses 2 and 3 of "There's a Way"). They can respond to the spoken narrative with force and energy ("No More Genocide," "Siph a Mandla N'kosi," "Singing for Our Lives"). They can set a tone or be a transition between one mood and another, or between one part of the play and another. ("Johnny, I Hardly Knew Ya'," and "I Am A Dangerous Woman," "It Is Important").

Where do you find poems and songs? For poems, look in specialized anthologies, find poets who lived/worked during the time you are researching, and find collections of their work, scanning tables of contents for titles that look relevant. For songs, playlists of songs from particular eras can be very useful. (Try an Internet search for "popular songs 1950s," for example, to see songs of that decade.) Collections of folk songs are rich sources. Timelines that list popular culture items, such as the book *Timetables of History*, can lead you to an era's mood-setting music.

Tuning Up Your Awareness

Once you have decided you are going to compile a Readers' Theater documentary on a particular topic, you will find that you are naturally tuned in when you come across appropriate material. Perhaps you see a program on television or hear one on the radio that contains elements you might want to research and possibly use. You grab a scrap of paper, make a note, and follow it up. Or you run across something on the Internet and bookmark the page. Or, as you read your daily newspaper, headlines jump out at you and you start a file of clippings. You meet someone in a social situation who turns out to be an expert in the field, and you are able to ask for specific details and suggestions. One thing that is crucial in this process is that you keep a research trail and notes. It is very frustrating to find a pithy quote jotted down in the margin of your newspaper, with no indication of who said it or where you heard them say it. If this does happen, don't give up without first entering a string of words from the quotation into Google or another good Internet search engine. Sometimes when you do this, your screen pops up with just the reference you need.

The Overall Arc

There is an art to selecting and arranging your material. The words (and music, if you've included it) comprise an emotional score that has an impact that is distinct from the impact of any one piece within your play. You will need to decide what voyage you want to take your readers and/or audience on and where you want to leave them at the end of the reading or performance. Do you want them in a thoughtful mood? Stirred to action? Ready to debate? Sobered by the size of a problem? Alarmed? Energized by images of survival and hope? All are legitimate options, though I confess I tend to prefer survival and hope over danger and despair. That is why, no matter what the most recent headlines or news items are in *Most Dangerous Women*, we always end with Gail Tremblay's stunning poem "It Is Important" and Holly Near's song of energy and resistance "Singing for Our Lives." The poem reminds us of a power larger than ourselves, of the wisdom held by our ancestors, of the overriding importance of love in the world. The song lifts us to solidarity and action. The interspersed quotations and poem excerpt, too, underscore a sense of possibility in the face of daunting difficulties. We do have the power to change things, we know how to do it, we can act as giants in what Gwendolyn Brooks calls this "giantless time."

So again, as you arrange and select your material, think not just of the flow of facts and ideas, but the flow of feelings in your play. Having said that, I also want to underscore the importance of keeping honest in your choices. In other words, if you use a narrative, song, or poem in a way that is counter to its intended meaning, you are distorting the documentary form. Be sure the larger original context of the words you choose supports the way in which you use them in your play.

Another element to consider when arranging your material is the need your readers or audience will have for emotional breaks from time to time. Too much of the same kind of emotion becomes something other than itself. What does that mean? If, for example, you have a monologue that moves your audience or readership to tears, and you follow it with another that does the same, and another . . . it won't be long until many if not most of the readers or audience members will be distancing themselves. Rather than feeling moved, they may begin to feel browbeaten or manipulated. Rather than feeling empathy with the character, they may begin to feel "enough already!" This is true for any emotion, not just grief and sadness. Emotions are by nature fluid, always changing in intensity and quality from one moment to the next.

However you arrange your material, you will need something that brings it to a closure. Remember that the last images in a sequence are always more powerful than those in the middle. What do you want your readers or audience to have in their minds as the final images/words? Think how different the impact of *Most Dangerous Women* might be if the final song, instead of "Singing for our Lives," were "Spell Against Sorrow" or "No More Genocide." The first would leave us lingering in grief, the second outrage.

Whether you use a song, a poem, or prose to conclude your script, the piece you choose should have the quality of summing up or commenting upon the whole play. One way to do this is simply repeat key phrases from main monologues or narrative bits in a vocal collage.

Suppose we were constructing a Readers' Theater script with music to explore the Great Depression. We might look to begin with cheerful music of the era and narrative to set the stage of exuberance and wild speculation that preceded the crash. Quotations from President Hoover might fit as well. Then, perhaps a sequence of headlines or timeline items that capture the intensity of the economic collapse. Personal narratives and songs (such as "Brother, Can You Spare a Dime?" and "Times Are Getting Hard") interspersed with facts and figures could follow, attesting to the bitter hardships but also the ways people found to persevere. Headlines of federal legislative and executive response, with some personal recollections of the experiences people had in government programs such as WPA and CCC might be the next section. Finally, a bit of looking back on the Depression from some distance would provide the opportunity to reflect on the consequences and the lessons we can learn, bringing closure to the play. The emotional arc of the play would follow the chronology, the moods people went through as they lived those hard times, from exuberance to despair to determination to relief to cautious optimism and sober reflection.

Emerging Secondary Patterns and Themes

As you accumulate material and sift through it, you may see certain patterns and themes emerging that you were not aware of at the beginning of the process. When we began to work on *Most Dangerous Women* in 1990, we had only one theme in mind: women as peacemakers. And specifically, the women of WILPF, the Women's International League for Peace and

Freedom. Why? Aside from the obvious reason that we were asked to create something to celebrate WILPF's 75th Anniversary and because it was the single women's peace organization of which we were aware that had lasted through the century, we were drawn to the fact that from the very beginning, WILPF had focused not just on being opposed to war (World War I in those days) but also on examining the root causes of war, in order to advocate social structures and political programs that would, by redressing those root causes, make future wars less likely. In fact, it was this wider view that garnered the "dangerous" adjective for WILPF's founders. So we set about writing our play focused solely on the women of WILPF.

As we read and researched, two other primary themes emerged. The first had to do with mothers and sons. Time after time in our editing process, we were drawn to written pieces that rooted themselves in the mother/son relationship. For it is this relationship that embodies the anguish of war. "They'll never take our sons again" swears the Irish woman to her war-ravaged husband. His generation had already gone to war, so it is their own sons, a new generation, that she is pledging to protect. "I didn't raise my son to be a soldier," sings the World War I era mother. The song lyrics capture the essential anxiety and vehement love of the mother who is watching her son march off to war. "What can we do to save others from similar sorrow?" Rosika Schwimmer demands to know. The tension of that relationships reappears, of the mother who wants to protect and the boychild who wants to seek adventure and "be a man" in Toyomi Hashimoto's devastating piece: "Still he bore everything bravely, and only asked, am I being a good boy?" At the beginning of Act II, Joan Cavanagh's poem has harsh words for the patriarchal powers that be about how they "sent our sons—yes sir, our sons—/to War." Still later in Act II, Mairead Corrigan Maguire speaks directly to that awareness of mothers when she cautions her infant son Luke to "refuse to have enemies." Helen Caldicott recalls the theme focus "If we can galvanize that instinct that mothers have . . ."

Over the years that we've performed *Most Dangerous Women*, this theme, once having emerged, has guided us in the selection of new material. In 1995, the situation in Chechnya was very much in the news. One set of stories told of Russian mothers following their sons to the front and literally reclaiming them from the Russian army. Given an array of headlines to choose from, obviously a headline over this kind of story would do double duty, by noting the conflict but also underscoring the theme. After September 11, 2001, I looked for an appropriate monologue to speak to both the horror of the event and the need to renew a commitment to nonviolence. I found it in Amber Amundson's moving letter to President Bush. Writing of how she wants her children to remember their father, Amundson evokes our theme implicitly if not explicitly.

Another clear pattern that emerged was the rhythm of war preparation and engagement. When a war is in the offing, the headlines of major newspapers are increasingly full of images of impending war. Wars do not suddenly appear. First there are tensions. Then accusations. Then threats. Then overt hostilities, which bring with them a self-perpetuating cycle that is terribly difficult to break. Perceiving these patterns gives us another of our subthemes: the way in which opposing sides in disputes are swept up into a feeling of inevitability. Senora Genoni's prayer in Act I speaks to this, as she pleads for the neutral countries to intervene before the warring nations simply exhaust themselves. Jeannette Rankin speaks to this when she attempts to break the skewed logic of war-thinking with humor and tells the person who asks how to get our troops out of Vietnam, "Same way we got them in. Ships and planes." When we update the script, we echo the rhythm of World War I and World War II headlines in capturing details of the current conflict in Iraq. If we are still performing *Most Dangerous Women* in the year 2025, I fear there could well be another conflict demonstrating that same rhythm, the one often called "beating the war drums." And I hope and believe that there will be women and men who remain voices of reason in spite of it, who call us to our senses and break the hypnotic hold that war rhythm seems to have on so many of us.

Often, concurrent with or directly following a war, there is represssion. The 1920s brought the title of our play, when benevolent Jane Addams was called the Most Dangerous Woman in America for suggesting that the starvation of German children would lead to another war. The 1950s and 1960s brought us McCarthy, HUAC, and FBI files that filled large buildings. Today, the war on terror comes with the attack on the Bill of Rights in the Patriot and Patriot II Acts. A third subtheme in the play, then, is the way in which the fear and insecurity that war engenders lays the foundation for repression in post-war eras.

A fourth recurring theme emerges. Women who claim their own power and agendas are ridiculed. Folly in petticoats. Lesbians and nudists. The taunt follows the fashion of the day, but the intent is the same, to diminish, to discount. Again, as we realize these themes, we become alert to them when it's time to consider new material.

These principles hold for any created work of Readers' Theater. As you amass material, sift through it, edit it down, you will find that in addition to the primary theme or focus of your research, there are secondary threads that reveal themselves. Notice them, encourage them, celebrate them. They give your play complexity and depth, but at the same time, they give it clarity. Whether your reader or your audience notices consciously or not, the coherence that these secondary themes provides is part of what makes the play emotionally and intellectually satisfying.

The Wisdom of the Group

While it is quite possible to research, compile, and refine a documentary Readers' Theater play entirely by oneself, it is, of all theatrical forms, perhaps the one best suited for group exploration. Having a co-author, or a committee of co-authors, or a classroom full of co-authors guarantees that there will be a multiplicity of points of view that are represented in the final product.

In one sense, the material you find as you research is your co-author, because you are drawing on many sources. Even so, it is helpful to bring others in on the process. In the early days of researching *Most Dangerous Women*, Nikki and I would each bring piles of possible material to our meetings, and Tamu Gray, an actress who had collaborated with Nikki on an earlier women's peace show, would join us. Each of us would read aloud the material we thought might fit, and the others would listen and give it a quick, intuitive thumbs up, thumbs down, or maybe designation. We rarely disagreed, but if we did, there was always that "maybe" pile where an item could be reconsidered. Sometimes when a selection was too long for consideration in its entirety, we would each read through it and circle the parts we thought most relevant and dramatic. (This editing process, and how it can be used in a classroom, is described more fully in *History in the Present Tense: Engaging Students Through Inquiry and Action*, Chapter 7.)

If you work on the material by yourself, you still will benefit from having a group of friends read it aloud before you finalize it. There are a few good questions to ask, and a few to avoid, to get good feedback from this kind of reading. The first questions are ones to ask yourself: When I hear others read this, does it flow? Are there places where there seem to be gaps in the logic or where something isn't clear? Is there an imbalance in the material such that it seems to be favoring a particular point of view that I don't want to favor? Places where the emotional tone stays the same for too long? How does it leave me feeling at the end? Is that the effect I want to have? The questions to ask of your friends are essentially the same. Ask them to focus on the material and your specific questions rather than telling you things like "I like it" or "I don't like it." General responses, even of praise, aren't useful at this point. Specifics are.

If you work on the material as part of a classroom project, be sure to allow plenty of time for the project. You may need to gather a lot of source materials together before you begin, to augment whatever research efforts the students will be making. You will definitely need to provide some structure and guidance. Having classroom discussions to sort out the overall intentions of your research, some guiding questions, and some guiding thoughts is important to create a sense of ownership of the project on everyone's part.

Setting clear deadlines by which certain phases of the project must be complete is crucial. Sorting out the various tasks associated with the project and making sure that each person in the class has a meaningful role to play is also of paramount importance.

If, on the other hand, you bring in the completed work for your students to read, you may still want to have some background materials available for them to consult either before or after they read the play. Biographies of key characters referenced, copies of newspapers with articles you've excerpted, albums of music with songs of the era(s) and themes represented in your play—these can help your students deepen their understanding of the material.

However you choose to do it, creating documentary Readers' Theater for your classroom is well worth the time you invest.

PART 2

MOST DANGEROUS WOMEN—THE SCRIPT

The history told in *Most Dangerous Women* is in documentary Readers' Theater format. Readers' Theater simply means that the script is designed to be read (and in this case sung) rather than fully "theatrically" produced. (It is possible to do a full production, with lighting, costumes, and more choreographed staging, but not at all necessary.) Not all Readers' Theater is documentary. Short stories, for example, can be arranged for performance as Readers' Theater. Documentary Readers' Theater is based, as the word implies, on documents—or more broadly, historical accounts. *Most Dangerous Women* takes its form in part from the Living Newspaper tradition of the Depression Era, when Works Project Administration (WPA) theater artists created theater from newspaper headlines. Headlines from nearly a hundred years of news provide the skeletal chronology for this play. Longer documents, including newspaper accounts, resolutions, editorials, minutes of meetings, letters, essays, poems, speeches, and interviews, comprise the muscle and sinew. Music might be said to be the heart of the play, as the musical selections capture and articulate with their own power the human emotions of war and peace.

Why is this such an effective format for teaching and learning history? Philosophers from Aristotle to Howard Gardner have recognized the power of theater that lies in its appeal to many senses and emotions at once. While a musical documentary Readers' Theater production lacks the grand spectacle of full costuming and staging, it still has the capacity to engage the intellect and emotions of audiences far beyond what occurs when one simply reads a textbook. From the audience standpoint, information is conveyed in a way that is entertaining and emotionally moving, appeals to our musical intelligence as well as linguistic, and engages logic and critical thinking by presenting a multiplicity of points of view. From the participant's standpoint, the learning is even deeper. An actor preparing to read a role, or several roles, must not only practice through repetition but must think about the meaning of what she or he is reading. We know that this combination of repetition and making meaning are conditions that promote long-term potentiation in the brain, in other words, learning. Finally, if the actors are involved not only in the performance of the piece but also in the research, selection of detail, editing, and polishing of the script, they are applying essential critical thinking skills and coming from a deep knowledge base. The very act of having to choose what is most important from an array of information means one has to pay the kind of close attention to the material that maximizes remembering it. So whether a person is engaged as a researcher/writer, a performer, or simply a member of the audience, documentary Readers' Theater can pack a tremendous amount of learning into the container of one or two acts.

The next section consists of the most current version of the script available at the time this book went to press. Because history is ongoing, *Most Dangerous Women* is never truly finished. Each time the play is produced, we rewrite the ending to bring it up-to-date. In 1990, when it was first produced, the Gulf War had not yet happened. Nelson Mandela was still in jail. The World Trade Center was still standing. And thousands of other events, large and small, were still waiting in history's wings. Groups using the playscript in a classroom setting may wish to do an extension activity of identifying headlines, news items, bits of monologue or essays that can be read as a coda to the published play. They, and groups interested in performances for the public, can contact Local Access, P.O. Box 22287, Seattle, WA 98122; Tel. 206-568-1195 to obtain updates to the script. Updates will also be posted on the Heinemann website when they become available. A one-act version is also available to organizations that wish to produce the play within the confines of school assembly schedules.

MOST DANGEROUS WOMEN

A Documentary, with Music, of the International Women's Peace Movement

by
Nikki Nojima Louis
Jan Maher

Original material written by Nikki Nojima Louis and Jan Maher

Conceived, researched, and compiled by Nikki Nojima Louis and Jan Maher with permission for use and adaptation of copyrighted and printed materials

Originally commissioned by

Women's International League for Peace and Freedom, Seattle Branch and performed at

Museum of History and Industry
Seattle, WA, September 22, 1990

ACT I

Johnny I Hardly Knew Ya'—Irish Traditional

World War I Headlines

The First International Women's Congress

I Didn't Raise My Son To Be a Soldier—Music—Paige Wheeler, Lyrics—Alfred Bryan

There's a Way—Jan Maher

Jeannette Votes "No!"

The 4th International Women's Congress

Headlines Between the Wars

Jeannette Votes "No!" (Again)

There's a Way reprise

Mildred Scott Olmsted Recalls

Die Gedanken Sind Frei—German traditional; translation by Arthur Kevess

Voices of Resistance

Toyomi Hashimoto Recalls Nagasaki

I Come and Stand—Original Turkish poem by Nazim Hikmet; English translation by Jeanette Turner; Music by James Waters ("The Great Silkie")

ACT II

"I Am a Dangerous Woman"—Joan Cavanagh

The 50's—Headlines

If Every Woman—Karen MacKay

The 60's—Headlines

The Civil Rights Movement

The Jeannette Rankin Brigade

The Ten Commandments on Vietnam—Dr. Martin Luther King Jr. and Coretta Scott King

Spell Against Sorrow—Music—Paige Wheeler, Lyrics—Kathleen Raine

From the FBI Files

The 70's—Headlines

"Dear Son"—Mairead Corrigan Maguire

As a Woman—Music–Joan Szymko; Lyrics adapted from Virginia Woolf

The 80's—Headlines

"The Situation in Soweto is Not Abnormal"—Mavis Smallberg

Siph'a-man-dla Nko-si—South African freedom song

The Women's Party for Survival–Helen Caldicott

Fresh Peaches—Alice Walker

The 90's—Headlines

Fact-finding in Iraq—Pamela Saffer

No More Genocide—Holly Near

The "Discovery" of America—Joy Harjo

Ja Sam Tvoj Svedok (I Am Your Witness)—Joan Szymko

Zlata Filipovic Writes in Her Diary

The Beijing Forum on Women

An Outmoded Proverb—Aung San Suu Kyi

Jody Williams and the International Campaign to Ban Land Mines

A New Century—Headlines

Children of Abraham—Arlo Guthrie

September 11

Barbara Lee Votes "No!"

Letter to President Bush—Amber Amundson

Ashes & Smoke—Linda Allen

The War on Iraq

Shirin Ebadi Wins the Peace Prize

Wangari Maathai Wins the Peace Prize

"It is Important"—Gail Tremblay

Singing for Our Lives—Holly Near, with additional verse by Jan Maher
and Nikki Nojima Louis

"Jane Addams"—Gwendolyn Brooks

ACT I

The stage is in darkness. Singers and Narrators 1 & 2 take places.

Sound: artillery fire, building to a pitch; then, suddenly, silence.

Lights up (sufficient for musicians to see their music) on Johnny singers & musicians.

Sound: violin introduction, drone voices: "Guns and drums and guns and drums. Guns and drums and guns and drums." Song: JOHNNY, I HARDLY KNEW YA' (Irish traditional).

SINGER 1:   With your guns and drums and drums and guns, haroo, haroo;
              with your guns and drums and drums and guns, haroo, haroo;
              with your guns and drums and drums and guns,
              the enemy nearly slew ya' -
              Oh my darling, dear ya' look so queer,
              Johnny I hardly knew ya'

Lights continue slowing coming up.

SINGER 2:   Where are your legs that used to run, haroo, haroo;
              where are your legs that used to run, haroo, haroo;
              where are your legs that used to run,
              when first you learned to carry a gun,
              Oh I fear your dancin' days are done,
              Johnny I hardly knew ya'

SINGER 3:   Where are your arms that held me tight, haroo, haroo;
              where are your arms that held me tight, haroo, haroo;
              where are your arms that held me tight,
              and kept me safe all through the night,
              How I wish you'd never learned to fight;
              Johnny I hardly knew ya'

SINGERS 1, 2, 3: You haven't an arm, you haven't a leg, haroo, haroo;
              you haven't an arm, you haven't a leg, haroo, haroo;
              you haven't an arm, you haven't a leg,

you're a spineless, boneless, chickenless egg,
and you'll have to be put to the bowl to beg,
Johnny I hardly knew ya'

SINGER 1:   They're rollin' out the guns again, haroo, haroo;

SINGERS 1, 2:   they're rollin' out the guns again, haroo, haroo,

SINGERS 1, 2, 3: they're rollin' out the guns again,
                  but they'll never take our sons again,

Four other women on stage, who have been providing the drone, now join in as well.

ALL: No they'll never take our sons again,
               Johnny, I'm swearin' to you.

The drone resumes, intensifies.

SINGERS 1, 2, 3: With your guns and drums and drums and guns, haroo,
                  haroo;
                  with your guns and drums and drums and guns, haroo,
                  haroo;
                  with your guns and drums and drums and guns,
                  the enemy nearly slew ya'

A beat of silence . . .

SINGER 1:   Oh my darlin' dear, ya' look so queer,

SINGERS 1, 2, 3:
  overlapping: Johnny I hardly knew ya...
                          Johnny I hardly knew ya....................
                                  Johnny I hardly knew ya.

Lights up full, including SR and SL where Narrators sit.

NARR 1:   1914: War breaks out in Europe. Russian women follow
               men to front.

Sound underneath: telegraph.

NARR 2: Unemployment and outbreak of war hit young German women hardest—eating war bread and being fed in cheap Berlin kitchens.

The women who have been singing in the ensemble take narrative lines:

VOICE: September: All able-bodied men in France gone to war, leaving Paris a city of women.

SHE crosses and stands in front of her seat.

VOICE: October: Antwerp falls to Germany.

SHE crosses, stands in front of her seat.

VOICE: December: British experience airborne shellings of cities. Is this the beginning of full-scale air attacks on civilians?

SHE crosses, stands in front of her seat.

VOICE: Denmark, Switzerland, and the Netherlands remain neutral.

As above, standing in front of seat.

VOICE: 1915: Surge of anti-German hostility runs throughout Britain. German shops are attacked and looted. Hundreds of top-hatted stockbrokers march to House of Commons demanding the internment of all Germans. Conscientious objectors disenfranchised.

As above, standing in front of seat.

VOICE: April: Russians lose 500,000 at passes.

VOICE: Disease spreads all over Serbia. 25,000 to 30,000 cases of typhus.

Remainder of cast enters, from stage left, each stating a headline as she enters, then crossing to stand in front of her seat. When all are on stage, double on lines as needed.

VOICE: Dutch journals talk of war.

VOICE: Bulgaria expected to join.

VOICE: British rout 15,000 Turks in Mesopotamia.

VOICE: French bombard El-Arish.

VOICE: Italy expects an attack.

VOICE: Kurds massacre more Armenians.

VOICE: French line creeps forward. Germans resist fiercely.

VOICE: Greek vessel sunk in North Sea.

VOICE: Seven million Poles in need of food. Polish mothers make soup of fir bark.

VOICE: Plight of Jews in eastern war-wrecked regions pitiable in the extreme.

VOICE: Minds of German soldiers unhinged by horrors of trench warfare. Asylums are full.

NARR 1: April, 1915: the ninth month of the First World War; 1,500 women from 12 countries converge on the Hague determined to wage peace.

They sit in clusters of 3s and 4s, as delegates. As each says her country, she raises a hand.

VOICE: Austria.

VOICE: Belgium.

VOICE: Britain.

VOICE: Canada.

VOICE: Denmark.

VOICE: Germany.

VOICE: Hungary.

VOICE: Italy.

VOICE: The Netherlands.

VOICE: Norway.

VOICE: Sweden.

VOICE: The United States.

They turn slightly to one another, in clusters, as if in quiet conversation.

NARR 1:   Ex-president Theodore Roosevelt calls them "both silly and base."

NARR 2:   Mrs. Lowell Putnam, sister of the president of Harvard University, says, "The women's peace party is the most dangerous movement that has threatened our people for some time."

NARR 1:   "A shipload of hysterical women," says the *London Globe.*

NARR 2:   "Folly in petticoats," adds the *Sunday Pictorial.*

NARR 1:   "All Tilbury is laughing at the Peacettes, the misguided Englishwomen who, baggage in hand, are waiting at Tilbury for a boat to take them to Holland, where they are anxious to talk peace with German fraus over the teapot." The *Daily Express.*

CATHERINE MARSHALL turns from the cluster she is in to address the audience in reference to the newspaper quotes.

CM: I want an educated and responsible public, not an ignorant and prejudiced public, which has taken its opinions ready-made from party newspapers.

Another woman, MARY SHEEPSHANKS, addresses the audience.

MS: We plunged into war relief work, all the while with the nagging desire to stop the killing, stop the killing. But it is not enough for women to do relief work. We must use our brains to urge peace among unvindictive lines, leaving no cause for resentments such as lead to another war.

A third, EMILY HOBHOUSE, turns out.

EH: I feel more than ever that men are motivated by greed, fear, and envy and are incapable of governing the world in a humane way. Put the British Foreign Secretary and the Kaiser each in a separate battleship and let THEM fight it out!

NARR 2:   On the evening of April 27, 47 American women, led by Miss Jane Addams, arrive in time for the opening of the International Congress. Aletta Jacobs, president of the Dutch suffrage society and first woman physician in Holland, is keynote speaker.

ALETTA JACOBS stands, addresses both the women on the stage and the audience.

AJ: We women judge war differently from men. Men consider in the first place the economic results . . . the extension of power. We women consider above all the damage to the race, and the grief, pain and misery it entails. We can no longer endure that governments should tolerate brute force as the only solution of international disputes.

NARR 1:   A thrill seems to stir the audience as the women of various nations utter sympathetic references to the sorrows, the hardships of their sisters.

NARR 2:   Dr. Anita Augsburg, Germany's first woman judge, speaks.

DR. AUGSPURG stands.

DR. A: Womanly feelings are above all race hatreds. The German women stretch out their hands for friendship and international love.

Several of the women hold out their hands to her as she returns to her seat. JANE ADDAMS stands and moves downstage, speaking to the audience.

JA: The large floor is completely filled with delegates, and the galleries crowded with visitors, both men and women. A solemn earnestness is evident everywhere. Flags of many nations, otherwise so conspicuous in international meetings, are completely absent. The keynote of every speech is woman's revulsion against the barbarity of the present war and her determination to work for the substitution of law for carnage.

NARR 1:   Jane Addams, probably the most respected woman in America, presides over the conference. She seems to have a certain presence which literally makes others more peaceful in her company.

JA: *(turns now to the delegates on stage)*

I find it a pleasure and an inspiration to preside over this first world gathering of womanhood in the interests of peace.

(back to audience)

The 1,500 women who have come to the Congress in the face of such difficulties must be impelled by some profound and spiritual forces. In the shadow of the intolerable knowledge of what war means, these women are making solemn protest against that of which they know.

She sits, while SIGNORA GENONI stands, moves DS. Another delegate stands nearby as her translator.

NARR 2:   Signora Rosa Genoni, the only Italian delegate, addresses the delegates in French.

SRA G: Nous allons priere pour le monde entier. Joignez-vous à nous!

TRANS: We are going to pray for the entire world. Join us!

SRA G: Et vous verrez que le monde entier devra nous écouter ainsi que les pays neutres.

TRANS: And you will see that the entire world must listen to us as well as to the neutral countries.

SRA G: Dans un elan de générosité ils comprendront que leur devoir envers l'humanité n'est pas seulement de sauve- garder leurs propres intérêts egoistes et nationaux ...

TRANS: In a spirit of generosity, they will understand that their duty to humanity is not just to safeguard their own selfish national interests ...

SRA G: ... mais aussi de ne pas attendre que les belligerant arrivent a l'épuisement avant d'intervenir.

TRANS: ... but also not just to wait for the warring countries to exhaust themselves before intervening.

SRA G: Et qu'ils décident enfin de s'unir pour trouver les moyens d'imposer la fin du carnage, la libération et l'indépendance de toutes les nations ...

TRANS: And they will finally decide to unite in order to find a way to end the carnage, a way to liberation and independence for all nations,

SRA G: et pour qu'a travers cette expérience terrible et sanglante ...

TRANS: and, so that through this terrible, bloody experience ...

SRA G: Les paroles du Christ, que tous les belligerants doivent connaître ...

TRANS: The words of Christ, which all the warring nations must know ...

SRA G: pour que ces paroles "pardon —fraternité—amour" puissent enfin embrasser le monde entier!

TRANS: so that the words "forgiveness, fraternity and love" may at last embrace the entire world!

TRANSLATOR sits. ROSIKA SCHWIMMER rushes forward, embraces SRA. GENONI, and turns the full force of her presence and personality on the audience.

RS: We must thunder forth a demand for stopping this war in such a voice as will drown the cannon's roar!

GENONI sits.

NARR 1:   Rosika Schwimmer, born in Budapest to an upper middle class Jewish family, was a forceful personality. She was someone you either loved or hated.

One of the women on stage speaks from her seat.

VOICE: No one can be neutral about her.

ANOTHER comments from her seat.

VOICE: By the standards of the day, she does not always behave in a way in which women are expected to. She smokes and likes the odd glass of wine. Traditionalists do not take to her bright, loose-fitting dresses which, being a follower of the dress reform movement, she wears without a corset or brassiere.

Other cast members react with expressions of shock.

NARR 1:   But only Madame Schwimmer can sweep the Congress off its feet. She suggests a minute's silence for those fallen in battle. The delegates rise in union.

ALL THE WOMEN stand.

RS: We have one among us who has learned that her son has been killed—and women who have learned two days ago that their husbands have been killed, and women who have come from belligerent countries full of the unspeakable horror, of the physical horror of war. These women sit here with their anguish and sorrows, quiet, superb, poised, with only one thought: "What can we do to save others from similar sorrow?"

SINGER moves downstage as piano begins to play accompaniment. Song: I DIDN'T RAISE MY SON TO BE A SOLDIER (Music—Paige Wheeler, Lyrics—adapted from Alfred Bryan, used by permission).

SINGER: I didn't raise my son to be a soldier.
I brought him up to be my pride and joy.
Who dares to put a musket on his shoulder
To kill some other mother's darling boy?

[Violin interlude.]

[SINGER sings verse a second time, building to an emotional pitch.]

I didn't raise my son to be a soldier,
I brought him up to be my pride and joy.
Who dares to put a musket on his shoulder
To kill some other mother's darling boy?

The women on the stage, as DELEGATES, come forward one by one, walking straight downstage from their seats to join her as they say their lines.

DEL 1:   We women, in International Congress assembled, protest against the madness and the horror of war, involving as it does a reckless sacrifice of human life and the destruction of so much that humanity has labored through centuries to build up.

DEL 2:   This International Congress of Women protests vehemently against the odious wrongs of which women are the victims in time of war.

DEL 3:   . . . urges the Governments of the world to put an end to this bloodshed and to begin peace negotiations.

DEL 4:   Recognizing the right of people to self-government . . .

DEL 5:   . . . urges the governments of all nations to refer future disputes to arbitration and conciliation.

DEL 6:   . . . urges the governments of all nations to unite in bringing social, moral, and economic pressure to bear upon any country which resorts to arms.

DEL 7: Since war is commonly brought about NOT by the mass of people who do NOT desire it . . .

DEL 8: Since the combined influence of women of all countries is one of the strongest forces in the prevention of war . . .

DEL 9: This Congress advocates universal disarmament . . .

DEL 10: urges that the organization of the Society of Nations should include a permanent International Court of Justice

DEL 11: and a permanent International Conference . . .

DEL 12: The people should take part in the conference . . .

NARR 1: Resolves that an international meeting of women shall be held at the same time as the Conference of Powers which shall frame the terms of the peace settlement.

ALL sit except the WILPF trio. SINGERS move forward as piano introduces the song THERE'S A WAY (music and lyrics by Jan Maher, used by permission).

SINGER 1: Teddy Roosevelt thought women had no business talking peace.
They are cowards said the Rough Rider; they're silly and they're base.
War's for men, it always has been, always will be; stand aside
While we brave male warriors take the planet for a ride.

TRIO: They shook their heads.
The ladies said:
There has got to be a better way.

There's a way to build a world based on dignity for all,
We are off to find solutions at the great Hague Hall.
We can eliminate the causes that lead the world to war.
There's a way to Peace and Freedom:
that's what we're looking for.

SINGER 2: Through the war zones these intrepid women made their way,
And they met and they envisioned a glad new day. They told the world that peace was how we all could gain.
Some said

SINGERS 1, 3:   "They're clearly dangerous,

SINGER 2:   Some said "They're just insane."

TRIO: They shook their heads.
The women said:
Will you join us in a better way?

There's a way to build a world based on dignity for all.
We have met to find solutions at the great Hague Hall.
We can eliminate the causes that lead the world to war.
There's a way to Peace and Freedom:
that's what we stand for.

SINGER 3:   Now the women weren't just talkers: they set off to see
all the heads of state. "Negotiate!" their simple plea.
But the war machine is stubborn and its nature is to grow:
When the U.S. joined, 'mid lonely voices, Rankin voted no.

Actress playing JEANNETTE RANKIN stands when named.

NARR 2:   Jeanette Rankin, Republican from Montana, the first
woman to be elected to the United States Congress.

JEANETTE RANKIN moves slightly DS.

JR: *(to audience)*
I believe that this first vote I cast is a most significant vote
and a most significant act on the part of women, because
women are going to have to stop war. I feel that as the first
woman in the Congress of the United States, I should take
the first stand. That the first time the first woman has a
chance to say no to war she should say it.
(to women on stage)
I want to stand by my country, but I cannot vote for war.
(to audience)
I vote "NO."

NARR 1:   She's a dagger in the hands of the German propagandists,
a dupe of the Kaiser, a member of the Hun army in the
United States, and a crying schoolgirl!

NARR 2:   Jeanette, you'll lose your seat in Congress.

JR: Never for one second could I face the idea that I would send young men to be killed for no other reason than to save my seat in Congress!

SINGERS: She shook her head.
            And sadly said

JR: (*speaking, in rhythm to music or singing, if preferred*)
            I believe there is a better way.

SINGERS: There's a way to build a world based on dignity for all
            And we women found solutions at the great Hague Hall.
            We can eliminate the causes that lead the world to war.
            There's a way to peace and freedom:
            That's what we stand for.

SINGERS sit down. ROSIKA SCHWIMMER stands.

RS: Those of you who know what it means to organize, know that to get that first international congress together from February to April, especially in wartime, when you cannot communicate . . . you will realize what it meant for those splendid women in Holland to get together an international meeting within that short time. People said "all right we see they are coming but they will come and they will fight and not accomplish anything." But they did not fight. Then the people said that there would be just some talking and nothing will ever happen, and when you realize what did happen, you will realize that this congress was one of the greatest things that women ever achieved.

SHE sits.

NARR 1:   The War Department must have agreed that something very important had happened at the Hague. In a post-war atmosphere of repression, it listed the Women's International League for Peace and Freedom as a Yellow Pacifist Internationalist Pro-German organization.

As NARR 2 names ADDAMS, BALCH and SCHWIMMER, they stand.

NARR 2:   Three WILPF founders, Jane Addams, Emily Greene Balch, and Rosika Schwimmer, were also designated as dangerous subversives. And what made them so dangerous?

JA: I cannot believe that the wholesale starvation of German children will lead to a lasting peace!

NARR 1:   This woman is the most dangerous woman in America!

EGB: We must transform economic systems in the direction of social justice.

NARR 2:   Subversive!

RS: We ...

SHE is cut off by NARR 1.

NARR 1:   *(with utter contempt)*
YELLOW PACIFIST INTERNATIONALIST PRO-GERMAN WOMEN!

THE THREE WOMEN look at each other, give up any attempt to speak, and sit down.

Music underneath: a few notes suggestive of the military triumph (in the style of "Over There").

NARR 1:   In the aftermath of World War I, the world powers meet to decide the terms of a peace settlement. At the same time, the Fourth International Women's Conference is held in Zurich. April, 1919: The American delegation, which now includes Jeanette Rankin as well as Jane Addams and Dr. Alice Hamilton, arrives in Zurich.

JEANETTE RANKIN stands, then is joined by JANE ADDAMS, Dr. ALICE HAMILTON, DELEGATE 1 and DELEGATE 2. THEY move DS, as if surveying the post-war scene.

DEL 1:   We are shocked by the deprivation caused by the blockade of food and necessities. To punish the citizens of a country we have defeated in war in this way is barbaric. It can only lead to bitterness and future wars.

JA: The day I arrived, while walking along the streets of Zurich, I encountered a woman who had been a delegate at the Hague Congress. She was so shrunken and changed that I had much difficulty in identifying her with the beautiful woman I had seen three years before. She was not only emaciated as by a wasting illness, but her face and artist's hands were covered with rough red blotches due to the long use of soap substitutes, giving her a cruelly scalded appearance. My first reaction was one of over-whelming pity and alarm. This was quickly followed by indignation.

AH: Food is a subject that has never left my mind for a day since I came here. The continuation of the Allied food blockade for months after the armistice seems almost a worse crime against humanity than the war itself.

JA: What are we about that such things are allowed to happen in a so-called civilized world?

NARR 2: Despite the constant reminders of death and destruction, the Congress is an exhilarating experience. There is a spirit of adventure, a sense of survival, of solidarity and com-radeship.

JR: The fact that we have never had peace need not deter us. Every day we see things we have never seen before.

DEL 2: It is unbelievably wonderful. There are 25 English women sitting with the Germans in front and the Irish at one side, all alike, engrossed in the common effort. The English leaders amaze everybody by emphasizing at every oppor-tunity that they are all socialists. Hitherto I have found it hard to take English women but this time I find myself their humble admirer. Never have I seen so generous a spirit in any group of human beings.

The GROUP sits.

NARR 1:   On the final day, Jeanne Melin, coming from a devastated region of the Ardennes, arrives.

NARR 2:   Lida Gustava Heymann rises from the platform to embrace her, saying: "In the name of the German delegation . . ."

HEYMANN's voice overlaps as SHE stands.

LGH: In the name of the German delegation, we hope that we can build a bridge from Germany to France and from France to Germany, and that in the future we may be able to make good the wrongdoing of men.

HEYMANN sits.

NARR 1:   Emily Greene Balch was quieter than Rosika Schwimmer, less famous than Jane Addams, but a powerful leader nonetheless.

BALCH stands.

EGB: I pledge to work with all my power for the abolition of war.

ALL acknowledge and join in her pledge. SHE nods at them, smiles, and sits again.

NARR 1:   It was at this meeting that the women determined that the gains already made should not be lost, and the name Women's International League for Peace and Freedom was adopted.

VOICE: We condemn the famine and pestilence in Europe as a "disgrace to civilization" and urge the lifting of the blockade.

VOICE: We denounce the harsh terms of the peace treaty that calls for the disarmament of only one side . . .

VOICE: that denies the self-determination of peoples, and enforces undue economic penalties. Surely these terms will result in the spread of hatred and anarchy and create all over

Europe discords and animosities which can only lead to future wars.

Music bridge suggesting the Roaring Twenties plays underneath next two lines.

NARR 1:   The Roaring Twenties

NARR 2:   Paris sees newest Futurist dances. The Aviator and the Shrapnel suggested to replace the Fox Trot and Shimmy.

NARR 1:   American Prohibition: First dry year called a success.

The women react with skeptical expressions.

NARR 2:   300,000 jobs lost in New York State. Unemployment growing.

NARR 1:   Says blondes induce eye fatigue for men. Optometrist describes new disease due to long staring at Fleshy Objects.

Another skeptical reaction.

NARR 2:   France resolves to make Germany pay and disarm. Many see only reparations solution as "holding a pistol to Germany's head." Hard terms of the allies may drive Germans to an uprising.

NARR 1:   England takes control of Palestine.

Music underneath next line suggests Depression Era.

NARR 2:   October 28, 1929.

                 (beat)

                 Black Friday, New York City. U.S. Stock Exchange Collapses. World crisis foreseen.

NARR 1:   1930: Last Allied troops leave Rhineland and Saar. Nazis gain 107 seats in German elections. France begins building Maginot Line.

VOICE: 1931: Financial crisis in Central Europe.

VOICE: 5.66 million unemployed in Germany.

VOICE: 4 to 5 million in United States.

VOICE: Jane Addams wins Nobel Peace Prize.

CAST MEMBERS nod acknowledgement to JANE ADDAMS.

VOICE: 1932: Gandhi sent to jail. All India quits work.

VOICE: Japan and China struggle for Manchuria.

VOICE: 1933: Japan withdraws from League of Nations.

VOICE: Soviets fortify area near Finland.

VOICE: Adolf Hitler appointed German Chancellor, granted
                    dictatorial powers. First concentration camps erected in
                    Germany.

VOICE: 1934: Revolution in Austria.

VOICE: General strike in France.

VOICE: 1935: Nazis repudiate Versailles Treaty.

VOICE: Mussolini invades Abyssinia.

VOICE: 1936: Spanish Civil War breaks out.

VOICE: Chinese nationalists, under Chang Kai-Shek, declare war
                    on Japan.

VOICE: *(cheerfully)* U.S. Employment picking up.

VOICE: 1937: U.S. Economic recovery accomplished.

VOICE: President Franklin Roosevelt signs neutrality act.

VOICE: 1938: Germany mobilizes.

Sounds of war begin to be heard: Marching, artillery fire, perhaps at a low level underneath the voice of Hitler. . . .

VOICE: Anti-Jewish legislation in Italy.

VOICE: Japanese bombers improve technique.

VOICE: 1939: Armaments race speeds on.

VOICE: Nazis invade Poland.

VOICE: 1940: German troops enter Paris.

VOICE: Nazi drive on Britain.

VOICE: Japanese attack French rail line.

War sounds intensify. Pace of lines also picks up.

VOICE: Holland gloomy on war and peace.

VOICE: Soviets accused of raid in Norway.

VOICE: War going well, says Churchill.

NARR 2:   December 7, 1941.

Sounds stop suddenly.

NARR 2:   Pearl Harbor Day.

NARR 1:   The vote to declare war on Japan was 82 to 0 in the Senate and 398 to 1 in the House.

RANKIN pops up on "1" ready to cast her vote.

NARR 1:   That lone vote was the voice of Miss Jeanette M. Rankin, Republican of Montana.

JR: As a woman I can't go to war, and I refuse to send anyone else. I vote "NO."

NARR 2:   Her vote was met with boos and hisses.

Other cast members hiss and boo underneath, then more loudly as she finishes.

JR: You should pay $30 a month, or whatever a soldier's wage is, to everyone and let everyone have a tin cup and bread cup and subsist on the same food that the soldier does, beginning with the president. For members of Congress who have voted for the war, let them receive not only the $30 a month, but also the honor of carrying the flag in battle so that they would feel that they are doing their bit.
        (a parting shot to the hecklers)
        You can no more win a war than you can an earthquake!

WILPF TRIO singers, from their seats this time . . .

SINGER: War came again, the U.S. joined (though Rankin voted no!)
        When Japanese-Americans were told they had to go to concentration camps it was the WILPFers first who cried "Internment's wrong!" and people said
        Song shifts to minor key.
        "You're on the other side!"

TRIO: They shook their heads
        and simply said
        There just has to be a better way . . .

NARR 1:   In 1933, WILPF's Munich office had been raided, and Anita Augspurg and Lida Gustava Heymann forced into exile. Contacts between WILPF sections had become increasingly difficult. Many sections went underground or into exile. Mildred Scott Olmsted recalls:

MILDRED SCOTT OLMSTED crosses DSC.

MSO: As a result of one of our congresses held after Hitler had come to power, I was taken aside by Gertrude Bacr and Miss Emily Balch. They asked whether I would perform a mission for the international, to go and visit the members of our German section who had not been able to come out and attend the congress. I was to go all alone and make contacts: I was given names and addresses and told how to do it. I had to memorize them all because it was dangerous to have them in writing. I arrived with picture postcards for my contacts, saying, "I bring greetings from your niece," which I delivered by hand. I remember being given instructions to go to the end of three tram lines, stand under a certain bridge and open a book. The moment I opened the book, someone joined me, and I was taken to a secret meeting of the League in the home of a woman doctor. They used only public telephones, and I was warned not to open my mouth of this if we passed anyone on the street. If anybody came to the door, the doctor immediately began lecturing on health foods and I kept my mouth shut. They sent me back with messages. One was "Don't let it be known that there are any WIL members here because we've been trying to persuade the government it's an unimportant organization."

NARR 2:   Everywhere, WILPF members did what they could to hold to their vision.

SINGERS come forward as music intro begins. Song: DIE GEDANKEN SIND FREI (Song: German traditional, English lyrics by Arthur Kevess © 1950 (renewed) by APPLESEED MUSIC. All rights reserved. Used by permission.)

SINGERS: Die Gedanken sind frei: my thoughts freely flower;
            Die Gedanken sind frei: my thoughts give me power.
            No scholar can map them, no hunter can trap them,
            No one can deny: die Gedanken sind frei.

            I think as I please, and this gives me pleasure.
            My conscience decrees this right I must treasure.
            My thoughts will not cater to duke or dictator,
            No one can deny: die gedanken sind frei.

            And should tyrants take me and throw me in prison,
            my thoughts will burst free like blossoms in season.
            Foundations will crumble and structures will tumble,
            and free folk will cry: die Gedanken sind frei.

The ensemble singers return to their seats.

NARR 1:   The roll of honour of wartime losses.

A woman representing each group or individual leaves stage or closes script and bows head as names are read. Ensemble singers should be among those who remain on stage.

NARR 1:   The two great pioneers from Germany, Anita Augspurg and Lida Gustava Heymann, die in exile in Switzerland.

NARR 2:   Eugenie Meller, president, and Melanie Vambery, secretary of the Hungarian section. Deported to concentration camps.

NARR 1:   Frantiska Plaminkova, outstanding Czech senator. Brutally executed.

NARR 2:   Six members of the Czechoslovakian section. Brutally executed.

NARR 1:   Marie Schmolkova dies in England.

NARR 2:   Rosa Manus of Holland, co-organizer of the 1915 Hague Congress. Dies in German concentration camp.

NARR 1:   Austrian, Czechoslovakian, Dutch, Hungarian, Polish, and Yugoslavian sections disappear.

VIOLIN plays "Die Gedanken Sind Frei" softly under the following: As each WOMAN speaks, SHE stands and moves downstage.

CZECH
WOMAN: Although our Czech section has been dissolved, we continue to meet at the Women's Club in Prague and work together to aid prisoners of war, internees, and the underground resistance movement.

POLISH
WOMAN: Our Polish section too has been dissolved, but all our members have gone into the resistance movement. Many women have taken Jewish children in to their families. On one occasion a large crowd of women flung themselves

like furies at a deportation train and rescued the children from the German soldiers.

DANISH
WOMAN: We Danes have maintained our membership of 25,000 throughout the war. Our monthly journal is published without a break. Educational and relief work continue and expand. Most of our meetings are held in private houses. Apart from one raid on our national office, there is no interference by the Germans. We even sell the WILPF "peace flower" to German soldiers, who wear them inside their tunics! We continue our protests to the Nazis against the persecution of Jews. In the teeth of Nazi prohibition, we continue to send food parcels to Jews deported to the Theresienstadt concentration camp, hopefully saving many lives.

2nd DANISH
WOMAN: Three hundred Jewish children who had arrived in Denmark the day war broke out remain here, cared for by our members. Almost every one of them has survived.

FINNISH
WOMAN: We Finnish members continue to hold meetings in spite of the German prohibition against peace propaganda. Although our section was broken up after the Russian attack, we continue to work on behalf of war victims with the cooperation of the Danish and Swedish sections.

NORWEGIAN
WOMAN: Our Norwegian magazine *Fred og Frihet*, which means "Peace and Freedom," continues to speak out against Naziism. Our chairperson has been imprisoned, but we continue our organization through underground channels.

JAPANESE
WOMAN: Our Japanese section was born in 1921 when my friend Riyoko Kadono and I met Jane Addams at a railway station. Now that war has begun, our section is banned, but we still manage to meet, sometimes in air raid shelters.

These remaining women sing:

SINGERS: And should tyrants take me and throw me in prison
            my thoughts will burst free like blossoms in season.
            Foundations will crumble and structures will tumble,
            And free folk will cry: Die Gedanken sind frei.
            And free folk will cry: Die Gedanken sind frie!

Sudden flashing of lights, sound of air raid sirens. Actresses on stage look around in alarm, scurry off the stage. (Narr 2 cross to SR wing.) Blackout, then flash of light, 2nd blackout. Sound of atomic bomb. As bomb sound fades, lights slowly return to reveal a lone woman, TOYOMI HASHIMOTO, stage center and NARR 2 at the NARR seat DSR.

NARR 2:   August 6, 1945. Hiroshima. Perhaps the darkest day in a
           dark decade. Three days later the United States drops a
           second bomb on the city of Nagasaki. Toyomi Hashimoto
           remembers that day.

TH: Though at each anniversary the skies over our city are blue
           and peaceful, the memory of that day in 1945 still troubles
           my body and soul. In spite of the wartime conditions, my
           husband and our little son and I lived a happy life. On the
           morning of August 9, 1945, I walked to the gate to see my
           husband off to work. My three-year-old boy, Takashi, went
           out to play.

           I was alone in the house when, in the distance, I heard an
           approaching airplane. "Japanese?" I wondered. I stepped
           outside to see my son running to me, calling, "Airplane!
           Airplane!"

           The moment we reentered the house, there was a blinding
           flash followed by a tremendous explosion. The roof of the
           house caved in, pinning us under a mountain of debris.
           Hours passed. I do not know how many. Then I heard my
           son crying softly and calling for mother and father. He was
           alive. I tried to reach for him, but a huge beam immobi-
           lized me. I could not break free. Though I screamed for
           help, no one came.

           Soon I heard voices calling names of neighbors. My son
           was bravely trying to crawl from under a heap of clay that
           had been one of the walls. When he turned and faced me,
           I saw that his right eye was obliterated with blood. Once
           again, I tried to move, but the beam would not budge. I

screamed so loud and long that I must have lost my voice. I called to the people I could see scurrying about, but they did not hear me. No one answered until the lady next door finally pulled my son out of the wreckage.

Happy that he was at least temporarily safe, I suddenly became aware of a sharp pain in my breast, left hand, and stomach. With my free right hand I grabbed a piece of roofing tile and scraped away the dirt covering my breast. I could breathe more easily. As I tried again to crawl out, I saw that a huge nail was stuck in my stomach. "Fire! Fire!" I could hear people shouting around me. It was either break free or burn to death. With a violent wrench, I pulled myself from under the beam. In doing so, I ripped the flesh of my stomach. Blood spurted from an agonizing gash in my body.

I was at last out of the ruined house. Still, my son was nowhere to be seen. Perhaps the kind lady next door had led him to safety. I had to search for him, but I could only limp slowly because of the pain in my stomach. I decided to go to a nearby hill, which was open and might offer some security. As I crept slowly along, people more seriously injured than I clutched at my feet and pleaded for help and water. I heard loud voices shouting, "Leave the old people! Help the children first!" All I could do was promise to come back with water, if it was possible.

On my way to the hill, I met a neighbor and friend. Looking long and intently at me, she finally said, "It is Toyomi, isn't it?" I knew that my dress was in tatters and that I was bloody and dirty. But now, stopping to examine myself for the first time, I learned worse. One of my ears had been cut nearly off. It and my whole face were caked with congealed blood.

"Thank heaven you're alive!" I heard a familiar voice saying. Turning, with intense happiness, I saw my husband, who was holding our son in his arms. We climbed to the top of the hill together, walking among countless corpses. On the hilltop, a kind man gave us bed sheets, candles, sugar, and other useful things. At once we began to try to do some-thing for Takashi, who had lost consciousness. After a while, as we dripped sugar water into his mouth, he awakened. He had already lost the sight of his right eye. Myriad slivers of glass were embedded in his head, face, body, arms, and legs. An air-raid alarm, still in effect, prohibited lighting candles. In the pitch darkness, my husband and I picked out as many pieces of glass from his body as we could find. So full of life and energy until that moment! Now blind in one eye and covered with blood and dirt!

Still he bore everything bravely and only asked, "Am I being a good boy?"

SHE stands quietly, head bowed. A YOUNG GIRL enters from SL; holding four long-stemmed white flowers. She sings the first verse of her song from her SL entrance position. Song: I COME AND STAND AT EVERY DOOR (Words by Nazim Hikmet, English version by J. Turner. Music by James Waters. © 1961 (renewed) by STORMKING MUSIC, INC. All rights reserved. Used by permission.)

GIRL:
        I come and stand at every door
        but none can hear my silent tread.
        I knock and yet remain unseen,
        for I am dead; I am dead.

SHE moves directly downstage.

        I'm only seven though I died
        in Hiroshima long ago.
        I'm seven now as I was then:
        when children die they do not grow.

SHE places one of the flower stems on the ground in front of her, and moves SL of TH.

        My hair was scorched by swirling flame,
        My eyes grew dim, and then grew blind.
        Death came and turned my bones to dust
        and that was scattered by the wind.

SHE places another flower stem on the ground, crosses to SR side of TH.

        I need no fruit, I need no rice,
        I need no sweets, nor even bread.
        I ask for nothing for myself,
        for I am dead; I am dead.

SHE places a third flower stem on the ground, moves further SR.

GIRL: All that I ask is that for peace
                      you fight today, you fight today;
                      so that the children of the world
                      can live and grow and laugh and play.

SHE places the last flower stem on the ground.

                      I come and stand at every door,
                      though none can hear my silent tread.
                      I knock and yet remain unseen,
                      for I am dead, I am dead.

SHE takes TOYOMI HASIMOTO by the hand and leads her off SL.

NARR 2:   At ground zero in Hiroshima there is a plaque that
                      promises: "Rest In Peace for It Shall Not Happen Again."

LIGHTS fade to black.

[END OF ACT I]

ACT II

The stage is bare. Actresses enter from alternate sides of the audience as they speak. The girl who joined the cast to sing at the end of ACT I is the last person in the lineup. Poem: I AM A DANGEROUS WOMAN by Joan Cavanagh. Used by permission.

NARR: I am a dangerous woman
carrying neither bombs nor babies
Flowers or molotov cocktails.
I confound all your reason, theory, realism
Because I will neither lie in your ditches
Nor dig your ditches for you
Nor join your armed struggle
For bigger and better ditches.

NARR: I will not walk with you nor walk for you,
I won't live with you
And I won't die for you
But I will not try to deny you
Your right to live and die.

NARR: I will not share one square foot of this earth with you
While you're hell bent on destruction
But neither will I deny that we are of the same earth,
born of the same Mother

NARR: I will not permit you to bind my life to yours
But I will tell you that our lives are bound together
And I will demand that you live as though you understand
This one salient fact.

NARR: I am a dangerous woman because I will tell you, sir,
whether you are concerned or not,
Masculinity has made of this world a living hell
A furnace burning away at hope, love, faith, and justice,
A furnace of My Lais, Hiroshimas, Dachaus.
A furnace which burns the babies
You tell us we must make.
Masculinity made Femininity

Made the eyes of our women go dark and cold,
sent our sons—yes sir, our sons—
To War
Made our children go hungry
Made our mothers whores
Made our bombs, our bullets, our 'food for peace,'
   our definitive solutions and first strike policies

NARR::   Yes sir
Masculinity has broken women and men on its knee
Took away our futures
Made our hopes, fears, thoughts and good instincts
'irrelevant to the larger struggle.'
And made human survival beyond the year 2000
An open question.
Yes sir
And it has possessed you.

NARR: I am a dangerous woman
because I will say all this
lying neither to you nor with you
Neither trusting nor despising you.
I am dangerous because
I won't give up, shut up, or put up
   with your version of reality.
You have conspired to sell my life quite cheaply
And I am especially dangerous
Because I will never forgive nor forget
Or ever conspire
To sell yours in return.

*The remaining actresses return to stage—alternating sides, overlapping lines. As
each returns, she re-states the poem's first line "I am a dangerous woman."*

NARR: 1945: United Nations founded.

NARR: 1948: UN Partition Resolution divides Palestine into
Palestine and Israel.

NARR: Rosika Schwimmer nominated for the Nobel Peace Prize.

ROSIKA SCHWIMMER comes forward.

RS: I hope that women will retrace their steps from the many blind alleys to which they have strayed in imitation of what we once called the "man-made" world; and remember that we sought equality for our half of the human race, not at the lowest, but at the highest level of human aspiration.

NARR: Schwimmer dies before the Nobel committee makes any decision. No Peace Prize is awarded that year.

NARR: The same year, Emily Greene Balch, winner of the 1946 Nobel Prize, has this to say to her exhausted colleagues:

EGB: Human nature seems to me like the Alps. The depths are profound and terrifying, but the heights are equally real. . . . It is not realistic to concentrate our attention on the recent revelations of the depths of evil to which human beings can descend. To do so leads to stumbling feet, weakness and discouragement. More significant are the revelations we have seen of moral courage, of devotion, of self-forgetfulness, of victorious human love and sheer goodness. We must draw a deep breath and fill ourselves with the fresh air of courage and confidence.

Entire cast takes a deep breath as music introduces the song: IF EVERY WOMAN (Music and Lyrics by Karen MacKay. Used by permission.)

ALL: If every woman in the world gets her mind set on freedom
If every woman in the world dreams the sweet dream of peace
If every woman from every nation—young and old, each generation
Puts her hand out in the name of love, there will be no more war.

NARR: The war to end all wars hadn't, and the war to make the world safe for democracy didn't. 1950: The Korean War.

NARR: Senator Joseph McCarthy advises President Truman that the State Department is riddled with Communists and Communist sympathizers.

NARR: Riots in Johannesburg against apartheid.

NARR: 1953: WILPF takes its place at the United Nations as a consultative organization.

ALL the women sit.

NARR: 1955: A seamstress in Montgomery, Alabama, takes the bus home after a hard day's work. When asked to stand in order to give her seat to a white man, she refuses. Rosa Park's simple act of insisting on the right to sit sparks the Civil Rights Movement.

NARR: Amelia Boynton of Selma had been organizing African-Americans to register to vote since the 1940s. She opens her home to other members of WILPF who come to help with voter registration campaigns.

AB: The night before the march we gathered at the church and talked with the citizens, asking them to walk with us regardless of the cost, even if it meant "your life." I was afraid of being killed, and I said to myself "I cannot pay the supreme price, because I have given too much already." But I also then thought, "Other mothers have given their lives for less in this struggle, and I am determined to go through with it even if it does cost my life." At that moment a heavy burden fell from my mind, and I was ready to suffer if need be.

NARR: The Sixties: Sirimavo Bandaranaike of Sri Lanka becomes the world's first woman prime minister; Indira Gandhi of India is second, and Golda Meir the third in Israel.

NARR: As more and more people go to jail for their civil rights in the U.S., more and more young men are sent to the jungles of Southeast Asia.

NARR: Jeanette Rankin resurfaces in the sixties, feisty as ever. In 1968, she leads the Jeanette Rankin Brigade: 5,000 women who march on Washington, demanding an immediate end to U.S. military presence in Vietnam.

JEANETTE RANKIN (DL) stands, as if at a press conference. Several REPORT-ERS question her.

JR: War is nonsense. Bring the boys back forthwith.

NARR: Might this not be interpreted as surrender?

JR: Surrender is a military idea. When you're doing something wrong, you stop.

NARR: But how?

JR: There's nothing to keep us from saying that we've run out of surplus war material and it's time to pack up and go home.

NARR: But how will we get the boys home?

JR: Same way we got them in. By ships and planes.

NARR: We have to protect ourselves.

JR: We'd be the safest country in the world if the world knew that we didn't have a gun. Men are not killed because they get mad at each other. They're killed in any dispute because one of them has a gun.

NARR: How can we defend ourselves if we disarm?

JR: Let me tell you a little story. A fellow from the country went into a bar one day and after drinking several beers, asked to be directed to the toilet. The bartender handed him a key, which the man accepted with wonder. "We've had an unlocked outhouse on our farm where I live for twenty years," he exclaimed, "and in all that time, no one ever stole a single, tiny turd!"

NARR: Ms. Rankin, if you had your life to live over again, would you do anything differently?

JR: No, with one exception. This time I'd be nastier. You know, I'm a bit frustrated. I worked for suffrage for years and got it. I've worked for peace for 55 years and haven't come close. I'm thinking of running for Congress again just to have someone to vote for.

NARR: At Rankin's side leading the Jeanette Rankin Brigade is Coretta Scott King, who says of Rankin:

CORETTA SCOTT KING stands next to RANKIN.

CSK: She is the endurance symbol of the aspirations of American women—the symbol of the aspirations for peace of all of us.

NARR: Two months later, Ms. King presents a statement at a WILPF news conference calling for negotiations and withdrawal of U.S. troops from Vietnam. Within two weeks, her husband Dr. Martin Luther King Jr. is assassinated. Twenty four days later, April 28, 1968, Coretta Scott King addresses a massive anti-war rally in New York's Central Park.

RANKIN sits, KING moves downstage.

CSK: My husband always carried with him many scraps of paper, on which he would scribble ideas for his speeches. I would like to share with you some notes taken from my husband's pocket upon his death. I believe he was preparing them for today's rally.

The Ten Commandments on Vietnam:

Thou shalt not believe in a military victory;
Thou shalt not believe in a political victory;
Thou shalt not believe that they—the Vietnamese—love us.
Thou shalt not believe that the Saigon government
     has the support of the people.
Thou shalt not believe that the majority of South
     Vietnamese look upon the Vietcong as terrorists.

Thou shalt not believe the figures of killed enemies
   or killed Americans.
Thou shalt not believe that the generals know best.
Thou shalt not believe that the enemy's victory means
   communism.
Thou shalt not believe that the world supports the United
   States.

(A brief pause. Then, with immense dignity and controlled grief...)

Thou shalt not kill.

NARR: January, 1971: WILPF members sign a treaty with mem-
               bers of the North Vietnamese Women's Union. As women,
               we are not at war with each other.

SINGER moves DSR. Song: SPELL AGAINST SORROW (Music—Paige Wheeler, Lyrics—Kathleen Raine. Used by permission.)

SINGER: Stream wash away, float away sorrow;
               Float away, wear away, bear away sorrow;
               Carry away grief;
               Mist hideaway, shroud my sorrow;
               Cover the mountains, overcloud remembrance;
               Hide away grief; hide away grief.
               Earth take away, make away sorrow,
               bury the lark's bones under the turf;
               bury my grief;
               Black crow tear away, rend away sorrow,
               Talon and beak pluck out the heart
               and the nerve of pain.
               Tear away grief.
               Who will take away, carry away grief?

NARR: The government continued to list the women of WILPF as
               dangerous in the extreme. A steady campaign of harass-
               ment, surveillance, and infiltration resulted in thousands
               of F.B.I. memos.

Two women stand, move downstage conspiratorily, as AGENT 1 and AGENT 2. They take up positions as if keeping surveillance on the audience and cast members.

AGENT 1:   F.B.I. memo. Regarding: Communist infiltration of Women's International League for Peace and Freedom (WILPF); Philadelphia. On October seventeen (name deleted) of Richmond, Virginia advised that five individuals distributed handbills on the Marshall Street side of the Federal Building, from twelve fifteen p.m. to twelve forty-five p.m. today. Observed among these individuals were Marii Hasegawa, Virginia State Chairman of WILPF and Phyllis Conklin, Richmond member of WILPF. Handbills distributed by these individuals reflect percentage breakdown of the federal budget. No incidents or arrests occurred in connection with this demonstration. Interested agencies advised.

AGENT 2:   F.B.I. memo: Subject: communist infiltration of the Women's International League for Peace and Freedom (WILPF). The female handed out a leaflet containing quotes from newspapers such as the quote New York Times unquote and quote Boston Globe unquote, concerning the quote bloodbath unquote in Vietnam. The leaflet asks that Americans speak out for immediate withdrawal from Vietnam. The demonstration ended at one thirty five p.m. without incident. Interested agencies are cognizant.

NARR: The '70s roll on. WILPF continues its thoroughly chronicled protests of U.S. intervention in Vietnam until our troops are finally withdrawn in 1973.

NARR: Power struggle in China after deaths of Mao Zedong and Zhou Enlai.

NARR: Last remaining European colonies in Africa gain independence.

NARR: U. S. backed coup overthrows President Salvador Allende in Chile.

NARR: 1974: "Someday," Golda Meir tells reporters, "peace will come, although I doubt that I will still be here to see it."

NARR: 1975: The United Nations declares the Decade for Women.

NARR: Indonesia invades East Timor.

NARR: 1976: Housewives Mairead Corrigan Maguire, a Catholic, and Protestant Betty Williams from Northern Ireland are the first women to win the Nobel Peace Prize since Emily Greene Balch in 1946. Maguire writes a letter to her infant son:

MCM: Dear Son,
            With ever so gentle steps, walk side-by-side with all the travelers on this 'thorny' path of life. They will differ from you in color, creed, culture and politics—but above all remember your fellow travelers have the same needs as you. Treat every man and woman justly and gently. In your life, Luke, pray to be a 'just' man. As you would ask natural justice of your fellow travelers, then you too must give 'justice' and respect every person's right to life. This means, my little son, that you must never kill another human being. It will not be easy for you to refuse to kill. It will take all of your courage to walk unarmed in a world which insists that you must have enemies. Stand tall and strong, armed only with love, dear Luke. Refuse to hate, refuse to have enemies, refuse to let Fear master your life. Remember always, Luke, people are more important than countries.

SINGERS move DS. Song: AS A WOMAN (Music by Joan Szymko, Lyrics adapted from Virginia Woolf. Used by permission.)

SINGERS: As a woman I have no country.
            As a woman I have no country.
            As a woman I have no country.
            As a woman I want no country.
            As a woman I want no country.
            As a woman I want no country.
            As a woman the whole world is my country.
            As a woman the whole world is my country.
            As a woman the whole world is my country.
            As a woman, as a woman, as a woman.

NARR: In Argentina, the government continues a terrorist campaign against the country's leftists. In a roundup of teachers, journalists, and political opponents, at least 9,000 are never seen again.

NARR: 1977: Women searching for their sons and husbands are forbidden by police to sit and hold public meetings. In defiance, they walk counterclockwise around Government House in the Plaza de Mayo. Soon, many of these women themselves disappear.

Violin reprise: last phrase of music from "SPELL AGAINST SORROW."

NARR: 1982: Sweden's first woman ambassador, member of the Swedish parliament, author, and disarmament negotiator Alva Myrdal wins Nobel Peace Prize.

NARR: 1985: Nairobi, Kenya. The International Women's Conference ends the United Nations Decade for Women. The WILPF Peace Tent at the conference is a center of heated discussion day and night.

NARR: Here Soviet and American women pledge to work together; here also Palestinian and Israeli women search for ways to begin a dialogue.

NARR: 1986, August 27: In South Africa, the Bureau of Information notes: "The Situation in Soweto is Not Abnormal."

Two actresses stand and move DSC as SOUTH AFRICAN 1 and SOUTH AFRICAN 2. Poem by Mavis Smallberg. Used by permission.

SA 1:   Everything's normal in Soweto today.
                      We reasonably killed eleven
                      They were making a fuss in the street
                      You know us,
                      We don't stand any fuss
                      Not us
                      So we typically killed eleven.
                      And wounded an average sixty-two
                      And you?

SA 2:   Went on a regular patrol to a school.
         Some children were breaking a rule.
         They burned their identity cards.
         White kids don't carry 'em
         Don't need to, you know
         Black kids don't carry 'em
         Don't want to, you know
         The whole thing was just about to erupt
         When we routinely went to beat them up.
         Cornered a few of 'em and rained down the blows
         Split one's head. She's dead,
         But nobody knows.
         Naturally the children ran all around
         So we just shot down those that we found.
         Bullets, birdshot, buckshot,
         What the hell? It's all run-of-the-mill!
         Saw this "comrade" walking alone,
         Shot him down before he got home.
         Ja, he died.
         You should've seen the ones that we fried.

Cast hums softly the melody to SIPH' AMANDLA NKOSI ("Oh, God, Give Us Power," South African traditional) underneath the following.

SA 2:   What a fire! What a blaze!
         Children crying, people dying.
         One woman got shot in the hip
         That really shut up her lip!
         Now she can't walk. Mmm, there was some talk.
         Ja, the situation in Soweto is not
         Abnormal today.

SA 1:   What's abnormal, anyway?
         What's monstrous, deviant, abhorrent,
         weird about gassing a baby
         Shooting a child, raping a mother
         or crippling a father?
         What's odd about killing the people we fear?
         No, the situation in Soweto
         is quite normal today.

Cast breaks into full song.

SINGERS: (ALL:)	Siph' amandla Nkosi. Wokungesabi. Siph' amandla Nkosi. Siyawadinga.

> Siph' amandla Nkosi.
> Wokungesabi.
> Siph' amandla Nkosi.
> Siyawadinga.
>
> Oh God, give us power
> To rip down prisons
> Oh God, give us power
> To lift the people.
>
> Oh God give us power
> And make us fearless
> Oh God give us power
> Because we need it.

NARR: Because we need it to redress the wrongs of the past, and to face the challenges of the future. Alice Walker observes:

AW: It must become a right of every person to die of old age. And if we secure this right for ourselves we can, coincidentally, assure it for the planet.

NARR: Helen Caldicott, author of *Nuclear Madness* and longtime member of WILPF, writes:

Helen Caldicott stands, moves DS.

HC: As Nikita Krushchev said, "In the event of a nuclear war, the living would envy the dead."

Now you will say, well what can I do? One thing I did was to start the Women's Party for Survival, because, as I travel talking about this, very often, it's the women who cry. Now I'm not excluding all mothering men. But, you know, women are very passionate, in fact, they very often drive men crazy because they're so passionate and emotional.

:   It's appropriate to be emotional.

Often, when I lay out the effects of a nuclear war, the person interviewing me on television will say "Aren't you being a bit emotional?" You can understand that that's a crazy remark to make. It's like . . . if I have two parents in my office, and I tell them that their child has leukemia and explain the prognosis, and they show no emotional response . . . I would get them to a psychiatrist.

It's appropriate to be passionate about our survival.

When I had my first baby, I knew I'd die to save that life. Now I had never felt like that about any other human life before, it was a profound revelation for me. If we can mobilize that instinct that women have to save their babies, across the world, we may survive. So I started the Women's Party for Survival and we're having a march on Mother's Day in Washington, wearing our Sunday best, even Republican ladies, everybody . . . because this is a very conservative issue. The ultimate conservative issue . . . The baby is our symbol . . . What we can do, when the Senate is debating the arms race, is to release hundreds of naked toddlers into the Senate Chamber.

We're on a terminally ill planet, you know that, and we are about to destroy ourselves . . . What I'm really saying to you is that if you love this planet, and I'm deeply in love with it, and you watch the spring come and you watch the magnolias flower and the wisteria come out, and you smell a rose—you will realize that you're going to have to change the priorities of your life—if you love this planet.

As Alice says . . .

ALICE WALKER stands as HELEN CALDICOTT returns to her seat.

AW: Life is better than death, I believe, if only because it is less boring, and because it has fresh peaches in it. In any case, Earth is my home . . . So let me tell you: I intend to protect my home. Praying . . . that my courage will not fail my love. But if by some miracle, and all our struggle, Earth is spared, only justice to every living thing (and *everything* is alive) will save humankind. And we are not saved yet. Only justice can stop a curse.

ALICE WALKER sits.

NARR: 1987: Palestinian Intifada, or uprising, begins in Israeli-occupied West Bank and Gaza.

PAMELA SAFFER stands and moves DS.

NARR: Spring, 1991: A fact-finding tour of Iraq is undertaken to assess the effects of the recent Gulf War on women and children. June, 1991, Pamela Saffer, a member of the tour and an American of Assyrian descent, shares her impressions.

PS: Mesopotamia: The Tigris and Euphrates. The Cradle of Civilization. 7,000 years of survival in the desert.

When they started bombing I wore black, couldn't look at colors, and thought I would never laugh again from the inside heart.
The whistle of bombs and people screaming;
My blood running in the desert.
I was enraged.

Sometimes I try to erase what I've seen.
I put my hand in front of my face
to erase it.
I cover my eyes sometimes.

>   The babies with skin stretched
>   over tiny bones;
>   mothers crying;
>   flies everywhere.

>   At Amuyah,
>   the mother who lost her four children;
>   the young father who lost his children and wife;
>   the grandfather . . .

>   Especially the grandfather . . .

They dropped 88,500 tons of bombs, the equivalent of seven Hiroshimas.

55,000 children have died as a delayed result of the war. Projected conservative estimates are that 70,000 more will die.

Though the Iraqis have withdrawn from Kuwait, sanctions against food and medicine remain in place. This in a country which imports 70% of its food.

Women are burying their children. For the Iraqi people, the war has not ended. The war continues.

But—being there is better than imagining, because I see that life goes on; that no one knows how the Iraqi families survived. But they did. And they will.

I face it over and over again: to be part of a good fight is better than sitting and crying.

SINGER crosses DSR to sing Holly Near's NO MORE GENOCIDE (used by permission) as PAMELA SAFFER returns to her seat and piano plays musical introduction.

SINGER: Why are the weapons of war so young?
Why are there always rich ones around when it's done?
Why are so many of the soldiers black or brown?
They say it's because they're good
at cutting other people down.
That's just a lie.
It's one of the many and we've had plenty.
I don't want more of the same:
No more genocide in my name!
People die all around the world
From starvation and greed all the time.
Some folks try to ignore the truth
by saying God and gun will provide;
In Kuwait, Cape Town and Beirut,
San Salvador, Greensboro, Belfast, Manila and many
     more . . .
It's a crime.
Do they think the fascist right will save the world in time?
They try to tell us so, but we've got to tell them no.
Tell them that's just a lie.
It's one of the many and we've had plenty.
I don't want more of the same:
No more genocide in my name!

SINGER returns to her seat.

NARR: 1991: Aung San Suu Kyi, leader of the democratic move-
             ment in Burma, wins the Nobel Peace Prize. Held under
             house arrest since 1989, she is unable to accept the honor
             in person.

NARR: Soviet Union collapses. Chechnya declares independence.

NARR: 1992: In this year of the Quincentennial, indigenous
             peoples of this hemisphere are joined by peace and justice
             organizations the world over declaring "500 years is
             enough!" As Creek poet Joy Harjo notes:

JOY HARJO stands, moves DS.

JH: "Discover" implies an assumption that something is lost.
             Something was lost. It was Columbus. But unfortunately,
             he did not discover himself in the process of his lostness.
             He went on to destroy Indian populations, and land, in his
             search for wealth, riches. The name, "America," too,
             represents a false face, a revised Italian name, superseding
             native tongues. Essentially, what we are dealing with here
             is a problem of perception. The Indian world is many
             cultures in one world in which human values are honored.

             Discovery implies that we are not present, are without
             history. It points to the source of the deep psychic wound
             that is in need of healing in this collective body—a wound
             of heart separated from mind, the lack of reverence for all
             life . . . For me, the act of revolution has to do with active,
             conscious healing of peoples, not the winning of wars, for
             there are never any winners.

             For Indian people, the "discovery of America" has been
             five centuries of heartbreak.

JOY HARJO returns to her seat.

NARR: 1992: Guatemalan Indian rights activist Rigoberta Menchú
             wins the Nobel Peace Prize.

NARR: First Earth Summit held in Rio de Janiero.

NARR: Ethnic unrest erupts in widespread portions of the former Soviet Union.

NARR: Ethnic cleansing in Bosnia-Herzegovina continues. The world watches on television.

NARR: I am your witness.

Song: JA SAM TVOJ SVEDOK ("I Am Your Witness" by Joan Szymko. Used by permission.)

SINGERS
(ALL):   Ja sam tvoj svje-dok;
Ja sam tvoj svje-dok;
Ja sam tvoj svje-dok.

NARR: In Sarajevo, 11-year old Zlata Filipovic writes in her diary:

ZLATA FILIPOVIC stands, moves DS.

ZF: Why is politics making us unhappy, separating us, when we ourselves know who is good and who isn't? I simply don't understand it. Of course, I'm "young" and politics are conducted by "grown-ups." But I think we "young" would do it better. We certainly wouldn't have chosen war.

ALL: Ja sam tvoj svje-dok;
Ja sam tvoj svje-dok;
Ja sam tvoj svje-dok.

ZLATA returns to her seat.

NARR: 1993: Oslo Peace Accords outline plan for peace in the Middle East.

NARR: 1994: Nelson Mandela elected first black president of South Africa.

NARR: 1994: Over 800,000 Rwandans slaughtered in a genocidal ethnic war. The international community fails to respond.

ALL: Ja sam tvoj svje-dok;
         Ja sam tvoj svje-dok;
         Ja sam tvoj svje-dok.

NARR: Russia invades Chechnya. Russian mothers follow sons to front, attempt to rescue them from forced conscription.

NARR: 1995: Beijing. The United Nations Fourth World Conference on Women is paralleled by a nongovernmental organization Forum on Women. Over 30,000 participants, including delegates from 189 countries and 3,000 organizations, take part in the conference and forum.

NARR: Reminiscent of comments from 80 years before . . .

NARR: Silly!

NARR: Base!

NARR: Dangerous!

NARR: Misguided!

NARR: Folly in Petticoats!

NARR: Theodore Dalrymple, writing in the *London Times*, comments:

TD: It was the lady from UNICEF who really began to worry me. "We must remember," she said, "that the girl child is the beginning woman." You do not talk of tadpoles as beginning frogs or caterpillars as beginning butterflies. When language is contorted in this fashion, especially in a political context, one suspects that something nasty is afoot.

NARR: James Dobson, leader of Focus on the Family, calls the conference "the most radical, atheistic and anti-family crusade in the history of the world."

NARR: Meanwhile, rumors are spread on the Internet that the NGO forum will be overrun by "lesbians, prostitutes, and nudists."

NARR: Nonetheless, the conference and the forum open on an inspiring note. Nobel Prize Laureate Aung San Suu Kyi, still under house arrest, addresses the gathering on videotape, smuggled out of Burma into China.

AUNG SAN SUU KYI stands, moves DS.

ASSK: There is an outmoded Burmese proverb still recited by men who wish to deny that women, too, can bring necessary change and progress to their society. "The dawn rises only when the rooster crows." The intelligent rooster surely realizes that it is because dawn comes that it crows and not the other way around. It crows to welcome the light that has come to relieve the darkness of night. It is not the prerogative of men alone to bring light into this world; women with their capacity for compassion and self-sacrifice, their courage and perseverance, have done much to dissipate the darkness of intolerance and hate, suffering and despair.

NARR: In closing remarks, Norway's Prime Minister Gro Harlem Brundtland notes:

GHB: When I first became Prime Minister fifteen years ago it was a cultural shock to most Norwegians. Today, fifteen years later, four year olds sometimes ask their mothers, "But can a man be Prime Minister?"

NARR: Gertrude Mongella of Tanzania, the conference's secretary-general, tells the delegates:

GM: The journey of a thousand miles begins with one step. There is no going back. There is no going back.

NARR: 1997: Nobel Peace Prize awarded to Jody Williams of Vermont, and the International Campaign to Ban Land Mines. In her acceptance speech, Williams tells us:

JODY WILLIAMS stands, moves DS.

JW: The landmine cannot tell the difference between a soldier or a civilian—a woman, a child, a grandmother going out to collect firewood to make the family meal. Once peace is declared the landmine does not recognize that peace. The landmine is eternally prepared to take victims.

Today Cambodia has somewhere between four and six million landmines, in over 50% of its national territory. Afghanistan is littered with perhaps nine million landmines. In the few years of fighting in the former Yugoslavia, some six million landmines were sown. Angola, nine million. Mozambique, a million. Somalia, a million. I could go on, but it gets tedious.

NARR: As a result of efforts by Williams and the International Campaign, 154 nations sign a treaty to ban landmines worldwide.

JW: It's breathtaking what you can do when you set a goal and put all your energy into it.

JODY WILLIAMS returns to her seat.

NARR: 1998: Massacres in Kosovo.

NARR: 1999: NATO begins bombing in Yugoslavia.

NARR: 1999: Massive demonstrations at World Trade Organization meetings in Seattle call attention to intersecting issues of peace, economic justice, and environmental protection.

NARR: March 8, 2000: International Women's Day. Dr. Nafis Sadik, Executive Director of the UN Population Fund:

NS: On the first International Women's Day of the new millennium, we are looking ahead with hope and determination. In all countries, women are joining together to call for recognition of the many things they do, in the family, in the workplace, and in society.

NARR: May: According to new research, childhood mortality in much of Iraq has doubled in the decade since the Gulf War and introduction of sanctions.

NARR: October: Israeli-Palestinian peace accord breaks down. Palestinian negotiator Hanan Ashwari asks,

HA: Who has the courage once again to intervene in the course of history and to change its direction from death and destruction to the promise and release of a just peace? Freedom, democracy, statehood and human dignity are rights that can no longer be put on hold.

SINGER stands, moves DSC as piano plays musical intro. Song: CHILDREN OF ABRAHAM (by Arlo Guthrie. Used by permission.)

SINGER: Children of Abraham, what's your story?
Killing each other for a piece of land.
Children of Abraham, this ain't glory.
You've got to walk together hand in hand.

You've got to take down the flags that just separate the people.
Take down the wire on the boundary,
Take back the words that were spoken in anger.
You've got to live just like a family.

Children of Abraham, I must be dreaming.
Rivers of blood running through your hand.
Children crying, mothers screaming,
just wasn't looking like the Promised Land.

You've got to take down the flags that just separate the people.
Take down the wire on the boundary.
Take back the words that were spoken in anger.
You've got to live just like a family.

You've got to take down the flags that just separate the people.
Take down the wire on the boundary.
Take back the words that were spoken in anger.

You've got to live just like a family.
You've got to live just like a family.

SINGER returns to her seat.

NARR: 2001, September 11: Terrorist attacks on the World Trade Center and Pentagon—3,012 killed or missing.

NARR: September 14: In the House of Representatives, the vote authorizing the president to use military force to retaliate is 420 to 1. The lone dissenter is California's Barbara Lee:

BARBARA LEE stands, moves DS.

BL: Last week, filled with grief and sorrow for those killed and injured and with anger at those who had done this, I confronted the solemn responsibility of voting to authorize the nation to go to war. Some believe this resolution was only symbolic, designed to show national resolve. But I could not ignore that it provided explicit authority, under the War Powers Resolution and the Constitution, to go to war.

It was a blank check to the president to attack anyone involved in the September 11 events—anywhere, in any country, without regard to our nation's long-term foreign policy, economic and national security interests, and without time limit. I could not support such a grant of war-making authority to the president; I believe it would put more innocent lives at risk.

I've been called a traitor, a coward, a communist, all the awful stuff. It's been quite difficult for me. But I still believe that I cast the right vote.

BARBARA LEE returns to her seat.

NARR: Amber Amundson's husband Craig Scott Amundson was among those who lost their lives in the line of duty at the Pentagon on September 11. On November 26, she stood before the White House and read an open letter to President Bush.

AMBER AMUNDSON stands, moves DS.

AA: Dear President Bush, my name is Amber Amundson. I'm a 28-year-old single mother of two small children. The reason I am a single mother is because my husband was murdered on September 11, while working under your direction. My husband, Craig Scott Amundson, was an active duty, multi-media illustrator for your Deputy Chief of Staff of Personnel Command, who was also killed.

I am not doing well. I am hurt that the United States is moving forward in such a violent manner. I do not hold you responsible for my husband's death, but I do believe you have a responsibility to listen to me and please hear my pain. I do not like unnecessary death. I do not want anyone to use my husband's death to perpetuate violence.

So, Mr. President, when you say that vengeance is needed so that the victims of 9/11 do not die in vain, could you please exclude Craig Scott Amundson from your list of victims used to justify further attacks. I do not want my children to grow up thinking the reason so many people died following the September 11 attack was because of their father's death. I want to show them a world where we love and not hate, where we forgive and do not seek vengeance.

Please Mr. Bush, help me honor my husband. He drove to the Pentagon with a "Visualize World Peace" bumper sticker on his car every morning. He raised our children to understand humanity and not to fight to get what you want. When we buried my husband, an American flag was laid over his casket. My children believe the American flag represents their dad. Please let that representation be one of love, peace, and forgiveness. I'm begging you for the sake of humanity and my children to stop killing. Please find a non-violent way to bring justice to the world.

Sincerely,
Amber Amundson.

CAST stands behind AMBER AMUNDSON, joins her in singing. Song: ASHES AND SMOKE by Linda Allen and Marie Eaton. (Used by permission.)

SINGERS (ALL):	We have been burned Burned by the fire And we are ashes, Ashes and smoke;
	But we will rise Higher and higher On the wings of compassion, Justice and hope.

AMUNDSON steps back as the rest step forward to form a single line singing a second time through.

ALL:	We have been burned Burned by the fire And we are ashes, Ashes and smoke;
	But we will rise Higher and higher On the wings of compassion, Justice and hope.
NARR:	October 7: US begins bombing Afghanistan. By December 20, a systematic independent study confirms that at least 3,767 civilians in Afghanistan have been killed.
NARR:	When the elephants fight, says a Lao proverb, it is the grass that gets trampled.
NARR:	Congress gives President Bush full authority to use force in Iraq.
NARR:	2003: Sand Brim travels to Iraq with Global Exchange.

ALL except SAND BRIM sit. SHE moves DSC.

SB:	The eve of war. Baghdad prepares to be assaulted and everyone is afraid.
	Forty percent of the people here are under the age of 16.
	Every night as I go to sleep I cannot help but think of the faces of children I have seen that day. I think of them

being put to bed by their parents and how it will be if the bombing starts. It is beyond the imagination that these little children are seen as so expendable, "acceptable collateral damage."

And I cannot help but think of that one young man who looked at me so directly and asked with such urgency, "Please help us."

NARR: March: U.S. begins bombing Iraq. According to Iraq Body Count, as many as 15,000 Iraqis, including up to 4,300 civilians, are killed in the first days of the U.S. invasion and occupation, in a campaign dubbed "shock and awe" by the Pentagon.

NARR: May: Bush declares end to major combat.

NARR: June: military patrols visit over 300 suspected WMD sites throughout Iraq. No prohibited weapons are found.

NARR: December: Saddam Hussein captured near Tikrit.

NARR: 2004: U.S. surprised at strength of Iraqi insurgency.

NARR: Abu Ghraib prison abuse revealed.

NARR: Iraqi interim government formed.

NARR: Government-backed militias in Sudan continue campaign of terror against civilians in Darfour.

NARR: 2005: Elections in Iraq, but insurgency grows.

NARR: In spite of peace agreement, violence continues in Darfour.

NARR: Cindy Sheehan camps in Crawford, Texas, demanding a meeting with President Bush. She writes:

CS: People have asked what it is I want to say to President Bush. Well, my message is a simple one. He said that my son—and the other children we've lost—died for a noble cause. I want to find out what that noble cause is.

NARR: Sheehan's peace encampment attracts thousands of supporters and revitalizes the anti-war movement in the United States.

NARR: U.S. death toll in Iraq passes 2,100.

NARR: Congress debates joint resolution calling for the President to develop and implement a plan for withdrawal of U.S. Armed Forces from Iraq.

NARR: Mohamed ElBaradei and the International Atomic Energy Agency awarded Nobel Peace Prize.

NARR: Iranian writer and human rights activist Shirin Ebadi, winner of the 2003 Nobel Peace Prize reminds us:

SE: If the 21st century wishes to free itself from the cycle of violence, acts of terror and war . . . there is no other way except by understanding and putting into practice every human right for all mankind regardless of race, gender, faith, nationality, or social status.

NARR: And environmental activist Wangari Maathai of Kenya, winner of the 2004 Nobel Peace Prize, notes:

WM: In the course of history, there comes a time when humanity is called to shift to a new level of consciousness, to reach a higher moral ground. A time when we have to shed our fear and give hope to each other. That time is now.

NARR: I wonder if Rosika Schwimmer, who had so passionately wanted a federated world, would consider that we had progressed? If her spirit returned and surveyed the scene, what would she say? She might be discouraged. But maybe she would see too that feminists from around the world continue to meet, talk, plan. I can see her now, calling for women the world over to take down the flags that just separate the people, heal the wound of heart separated from mind, create a world of compassion, justice, and hope.

This is when knowing feminist history is so wonderful. It makes us feel less lonely and keeps us going. Poet Gail Tremblay writes:

MUSIC transition: Native American flute or percussion. Four actresses downstage. Poem: IT IS IMPORTANT by Gail Tremblay. (Used by permission of Calyx Books.)

NARR: On dark nights, when thoughts fly like nightbirds
Looking for prey, it is important to remember
to bless with names every creature that comes
to mind; to sing a thankful song and hold
the magic of the whole creation close in the heart,
to watch light dance and know the sacred is alive.

NARR: On dark nights, when owls watch, their eyes
gleaming in the black expanse of starless sky,
it is important to gather the medicine bones,
the eagle feathers, the tobacco bundles, the braided
sweetgrass, the cedar, and the sage, and pray
the world will heal and breath feed the plants
that care for the nations keeping the circle whole.

NARR: On dark nights, when those who think only of themselves
conjure over stones and sing spells to feed their wills,
it is important to give gifts and to love everything
that shows itself as good. It is time to turn
to the Great Mystery and know the Grandfathers have
mercy on us that we may help the people to survive.

NARR: On dark nights, when confusion makes those who envy
hate and curse the winds, face the four directions
and mumble names, it is important to stand
and see that our only work is to give what others
need, that everything that touches us is a holy
gift to teach us we are loved. When sun rises,
and light surrounds life making blessings grow,
it is important to praise its coming, and exhale
letting all we hold inside our lungs travel east
and mix its power with the air; it is important to praise
dawn's power breathing in and know we live in good
relation to all creation

ALL FOUR: and sing what we must sing.

Piano plays musical intro as the rest of the cast stands to sing: SINGING FOR OUR LIVES by Holly Near with additional final verse by Jan Maher and Nikki Nojima Louis. (Used by permission.)

CAST: We are a gentle angry people,
                 and we are singing, singing for our lives.

                 We are a gentle angry people,
                 and we are singing, singing for our lives.

Cast hums the last line again underneath EDITH BALLANTYNE'S inter-jected line.

EB: I guess I am optimistic. People made this world the way it is; people can change it.

CAST: We are young and old together,
                 and we are singing, singing for our lives.

                 We are young and old together,
                 and we are singing, singing for our lives.

                 We are straight and gay together,
                 and we are singing, singing for our lives,

                 We are straight and gay together,
                 and we are singing, singing for our lives.

As before, humming underneath JANET BRUIN'S interjected line.

JB: Working together, each in our own community and each in our own country, we can do it. I'm sure.

Cast resumes singing, in full harmony.

CAST: We are a land of many colors,
                 and we are singing, singing for our lives,

                 We are a land of many colors,
                 and we are singing, singing for our lives.

Cast hums entire melody through one time underneath BETTY MCINTOSH'S interjected line and the narrative line, and fades out at the GWENDOLYN BROOKS poem excerpt . . .

BM: Anyhow, there isn't an alternative—we must keep going. There's always another injustice. Just when you think you've finished, you see something happening and you say, "Let's see what we can do about this one."

NARR: A benediction from a poem by Gwendolyn Brooks, called "Jane Addams:"

Actress reading GWENDOLYN BROOKS steps DSC.

GB: I am saying to the giantless time—
to the young and yammering, to the
old and corrected,

SHE looks to the young girl who sang "I Come and Stand" and read ZLATA FILIPOVIC.

well, chiefly to Children Coming
Home
with worried faces and questions
about world-survival—

"Go ahead and live your life.
You might be surprised. The world
might continue."

SHE refers the rest of the lines to her fellow cast members and to the audience.

GB, cont'd: Go on with your preparations,
moving among the quick and the
dead;
nourishing here, there;
pressing a hand,
among the ruins,
and among the seeds of restoration.
So speaks a giant, Jane.

Brief piano introduction ("Singing for our lives"). Cast places scripts on seats, joins hands, and resumes singing with great energy.

ALL: We are the world's most dangerous women,
and we are singing, singing for our lives,

We are the world's most dangerous women,
and we are singing, singing for our lives.

CAST sings verse another time, walking to edge of stage, raising clasped hands into the air on final "Singing for Our Lives."

We are the world's most dangerous women,
and we are singing, singing for our lives,

We are the world's most dangerous women,
And we are singing, singing for our lives.

END OF SHOW

Production Notes:

Casting

Character names are noted when lines are direct quotes. Otherwise, narrative lines are indicated as follows: In Act I, two primary narrators are named Narr 1 and Narr 2. Other narrative lines are named Voice. In Act II, all narrative lines are named Narr. Cast may range in size from nine to as many as may be available (productions of *Most Dangerous Women* have had up to 26 women in a single cast). Emily Greene Balch, Rosika Schwimmer, and Jeannette Rankin appear in both Act I and Act II. Audiences will be able to follow these characters, as well as the character of Jane Addams, more easily if the actresses playing these roles do not have other significant monologue assignments in Act I. For the same reason, actresses with monologues in Act I should not be assigned Act I narrative roles and vice versa. Singers are referred to as either Singer (for solo pieces) or Singers (for ensemble pieces). When lines are divided among Singers, it is indicated by assigning a number to each singer (Singer 1, Singer 2, Singer 3, etc.).

Names

There are numerous names that are difficult to pronounce. Readers are advised to research proper pronunciation, make pronunciation notes in their scripts as needed, and practice correct phonetic reading prior to performance.

Accents

In most readings and productions, there will be some people who feel comfortable attempting character accents and others who will not. Our general guideline is to keep the accents very subtle, so they don't distract from the words or call attention to a discrepancy of some actresses using accents and others not doing so.

Costumes

In Act I, skirts or dresses. Browns, blues, greens, oranges, blacks, with the exception of the actress who plays Rosika Schwimmer, who can (and should) wear something brighter.

In Act II, skirts, dresses, or pants outfits. Same color scheme.

(The color scheme is suggested by the NASA photograph of earth from outer space.)

Staging

The script suggests some staging. Minimally, it is suggested that actresses with character monologues stand. A few sound effects and simple lighting effects are suggested, but not required. Placement of musicians depends upon the size and shape of the performing area, the technical capabilities, and the number of musicians and cast members. One possible arrangement is in the diagram below.

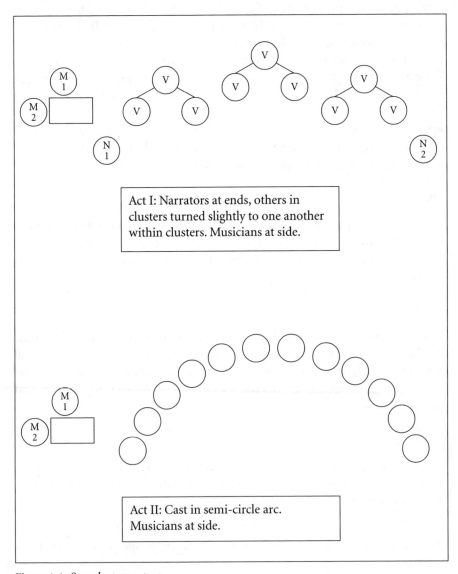

Act I: Narrators at ends, others in clusters turned slightly to one another within clusters. Musicians at side.

Act II: Cast in semi-circle arc. Musicians at side.

Figure 4–1 *Sample stage set-up.*

Appendix A

The Women and Men of
Most Dangerous Women

There are words from a great many women and a few men in *Most Dangerous Women*. Their brief biographies are listed here, along with suggestions—in most cases—for where you might begin to learn more about their work.

Jane Addams (1860–1935)

Jane Addams was born in 1860, the daughter of relative privilege. In 1889 she founded the first settlement house (Hull House) in a Chicago immigrant neighborhood. Hull House offered day care, kindergarten, employment services, and cooking and other classes to help recent immigrants learn how to get along in this country. Addams supported women's suffrage and the founding of the American Civil Liberties Union. During World War I, she became a peace activist and remained so after the war. In 1931, she was awarded the Nobel Peace Prize. She died in 1935. To read more about Jane Addams, see www.uic.edu/jaddams/hull/ja_bio.html.

Linda Allen

Linda Allen is a songwriter, song collector, and teacher. Her songs have been sung and/or recorded by numerous artists and have appeared in publications such as *Sing Out!* and *Broadside*. She was resident songwriter for the State of Washington's Centennial Project in 1988/89 and worked extensively with the Washington Women's Heritage Project. You can learn more about her work at www.lindasongs.com.

Amber Amundson

Amber Amundson's first letter about September 11, 2001, was published in the *Chicago Tribune* on September 25, 2001. Her open letter to President Bush was delivered November 24, 2001, as part of A Walk for Healing and Peace from Arlington National Cemetery to Ground Zero in New York City, organized with the help of Voices in the Wilderness. In January 2002 she was featured on PBS's *NOW* with Bill Moyers. She and her brothers-in-law Barry and Ryan Amundson are among the founders of Peaceful Tomorrows, an organization begun by family members of victims of the 9/11 attacks who have united to turn their grief into action for peace. You can learn more about their efforts at www.peacefultomorrows.org.

Hanan Ashwari (1946–)

Hanan Ashwari was born in 1946 and grew up in Ramallah in the Palestinian West Bank region. She studied English and literature, obtaining a doctorate from the University of Virginia. Returning home in 1973, she established the Department of English at Birzeit University on the West Bank and was Dean of the Faculty of Arts from 1986–1990. In 1991 she was appointed by Yasser Arafat as official spokesperson of the Palestinian Delegation to the Middle East Peace Process. She became a member of the Palestinian Legislative Council, but resigned in 1998. That same year, she founded MIPTAH–The Palestinian Initiative for the Promotion of Global Dialogue and Democracy.

Anita Augsburg (1857–1943)

Anita Augsburg was a German feminist and pacifist, and the first woman attorney in Germany. She participated in the international abolitionist movement and worked for suffrage for women in Germany. Augsburg was a delegate to the First International Congress at the Hague. When the Nazis came to power in Germany she went to Switzerland with her friend and colleague Lida Gustava Heymann. She worked as a journalist in Switzerland. For more information on her legal career, see *Women in Law—A Bibliographical Sourcebook* (Edited by R. M. Salokar and M. L. Volcansek, Eds.).

Emily Greene Balch (1867–1961)

Emily Greene Balch was a member of the first graduating class of Bryn Mawr College in 1889. A professor of economics and sociology at Wellesley College, she spoke out for women's suffrage, racial justice, control of child labor, and improved wages and working conditions for laborers. Balch was the first international secretary of Women's International League for Peace and Freedom (WILPF) and first editor of the League's magazine, *Pax International*. She was fired from her position at Wellesley for her peace activism. She won the Nobel Peace Prize in 1946. To read more about Emily Green Balch, see http://nobelprize.org/peace/laureates/1946/balch-bio.html.

Edith Ballantyne

Edith Ballantyne was a refugee from Naziism, leaving Sudetan when the Germans annexed it. Her family was settled in Canada in 1939. In 1948, she married and moved to Switzerland, where she worked for the World Health Organization and raised a family. She was international secretary of WILPF in 1969, and in 1973 was elected secretary of the NGO subcommittee on Racism and Decolonization. She was international president of WILPF from 1993 to 1998. To read more about Edith Ballantyne, see *Women for All Seasons*.

Sirimavo Bandaranaike (1916–2000)

Sirimavo Bandaranaike was three times prime minister of Sri Lanka. A widow of Prime Minister Solomon Bandaranaike, who was assassinated in 1959, she became the world's first elected woman prime minister in 1960. She declared the country a republic in 1972, changing its name from Ceylon to Sri Lanka.

Amelia Boynton (1911–)

Amelia Boynton was born in Georgia in 1911. Along with her husband S. W. Boynton, she fought for justice and civil rights from the 1930s on. In 1964, she became the first African American woman to seek a seat in Congress from Alabama. On March 7, 1965, marching at the front of the "Bloody Sunday" march for voting rights from Selma to Montgomery, Alabama, she was gassed, beaten, and left for dead. Images of her treatment galvanized international support for the Civil Rights Movement. Today, she is Vice Chairman of the Schiller Institute. For more about Amelia Boynton, see www.schiller institute.org/biographys/bio_amelia_new.html.

Sand Brim

Sand Brim is an attorney and businesswoman from Los Angeles, California. She is owner of Culture Shop Gallery, a contemporary craft gallery in Santa Monica, California. She served as an aide for Coretta Scott King in the early 1970s, lived and worked on the Pine Ridge Indian Reservation as a member of the Wounded Knee Legal Defense Committee, was a union organizer and educator in the 1980s, and Director of Medical Aid for El Salvador. She represented children and families in Juvenile Dependency Court for over 11 years. She is currently working with community organizations in Venice, California, and devoting a great deal of time and effort to ending the war in Iraq.

Gwendolyn Brooks (1917–2000)

Though born in Kansas, Gwendolyn Brooks moved to Chicago shortly after her birth and lived there until her death in 2000. In 1950 Ms. Brooks became the first African American to win a Pulitzer Prize. She was appointed poet laureate for the State of Illinois in 1968. Her books include the novel *Maude Martha*, her autobiography *Report from Part One* (written when she was 50), and many volumes of poetry, including *Bronzeville Boys and Girls* and *In the Mecca*. To read more about Gwendolyn Brooks, see www.poets.org/poet.php /prmPID/165. This site also includes links to several of her poems.

Janet Bruin

Janet Bruin grew up in Philadelphia. A social worker by training, she moved to Zurich in 1978 and began editing *Pax et Libertas*, the WILPF quarterly. She was instrumental in reviving the Swiss section of WILPF. You can read more about Janet Bruin in *Women for All Seasons*.

Gro Harlem Brundtland (1939–)

Gro Harlem Brundtland trained as a medical doctor and spent ten years as a physician and scientist before entering public office. From 1965 to 1975 she worked in Norway's Ministry of Health on children's health issues. In 1981, at the age of 41, Gro Harlem Brundtland became Norway's youngest and first woman prime minister. She served 10 years in that office. From 1998 to 2003 she was director general of the World Health Organization. For more information about Dr. Brundtland, see www.who.int/dg/brundtland/bruntland/en/.

Alfred Bryan (1871–1958)

Alfred Bryan was born in Canada but moved to the United States early in his musical career. He was a charter member of ASCAP. He collaborated on several Broadway musicals and also wrote songs for film scores. Two of his best-known songs are "Peg O' My Heart" and "Come Josephine in my Flying Machine." You can read more about Alfred Bryan and his work at www.songwritershalloffame.org/exhibit_home_page.asp?exhibitId=326.

Helen Caldicott (1938–)

Helen Caldicott was born in Melbourne, Australia, in 1938. She received her medical degree in 1961, taught pediatrics at Harvard Medical School, and served on the staff of Children's Hospital Medical Center in Boston until 1980 when she resigned to devote herself full time to the prevention of nuclear war. She is co-founder of Physicians for Social Responsibility, founder of Women's Action for Nuclear Disarmament, and founder/president of the Nuclear Policy Research Institute. Dr. Caldicott is author of numerous books, most recently *The New Nuclear Danger: George Bush's Military Industrial Complex* (The New Press, 2001). She has been nominated for the Nobel Peace Prize and received the Lannan Foundation 2003 Prize for Cultural Freedom. You can learn more about Dr. Caldicott at her website, http://www.helencaldicott.com.

Joan Cavanagh (1955–)

Joan Cavanagh is a longtime peace and justice activist and advocate. She is 51 years old, and lives in New Haven, where she works as an archivist, historian, and writer. She wrote the poem used here 30 years ago, just after being released from 52 days in jail for a nonviolent action against the U.S. war in Vietnam.

Theodore Dalrymple

Theodore Dalrymple, a physician and psychiatrist who practices in England, is a contributing editor to the Manhattan Institute's City Journal. His columns appear in the *London Spectator* and the *Daily Telegraph*. His books include *Mass Listerial, Life at the Bottom: The World View that Makes the Underclass,* and *Our Culture, What's Left of It: The Mandarins and The Masses.*

James Dobson

James Dobson is founder and chairman of Focus on the Family. For 14 years, he was Associate Clinical Professor of pediatrics at the University of Southern California School of Medicine. He is a radio commentator and author whose books include *Dare to Discipline, Marriage under Fire,* and *Emotions: Can You Trust Them?*

Shirin Ebadi (1947–)

Shirin Ebadi was born in 1947 in Iran. She studied law at Tehran University, receiving a doctorate in 1971. She was the first woman in Iran to become a judge, but was dismissed from her post after the Islamic Revolution in 1979. In 1992, she set up her own legal practice. She is an author of several books and articles, teaches at the university level, has led several research projects for the United Nations Children's Emergency Fund office in Tehran, is co-founder of the Association for Support of Children's Rights, president of the Human Rights Defence Centre, writes, and lectures widely on human rights and children's rights issues. Ebadi was awarded the 2003 Nobel Peace Prize. For more information about her, see http://nobelprize.org/peace/laureates/2003/ebadi-bio.html.

Zlata Filipovic

At 11, Zlata Filipovic authored *Zlata's Diary: An Eleven Year Old's Life in Sarajevo During the Civil War.* Since then, she has lived with her family in exile in Paris and Dublin. She established the Zlata Fund to benefit children displaced or orphaned by war. Her diary has been adapted to stage and has been performed in Ireland and Scotland. She and her parents tour the world to promote peace. You can find out more about her at www.penguin.co.uk/nf/Author/AuthorPage/0,,0_1000010817,00.html.

Indira Gandhi (1917–1984)

Indira Gandhi was the daughter of India's first prime minister, Jawaharlal Nehru. As a child, she participated in resistance against British occupation of India. She was the fourth woman to be elected president of the Indian National Congress and in 1967 was the second woman in the world to be elected prime minister of her country. Her years in power were controversial. In 1975 she declared a state of emergency, limiting the freedoms of Indian citizens, and in 1977 she was voted out of office. In 1980 she regained her position as prime minister but in 1984 was assassinated by one of her bodyguards. You can learn more about Indira Gandhi at www.indianchild.com/indira_gandhi.htm.

Rosa Genoni (1867–1954)

Rosa Genoni was an Italian costume designer and delegate to the First International Congress at The Hague and the Fourth International Congress in Zurich. Along with Jane Addams and Aletta Jacobs, Rosa Genoni went to Austro-Hungary, Belgium, Britain, France, Germany, Italy, and Switzerland to visit heads of state to petition for an end to World War I. She also worked within Italy to promote anti-war sentiment.

Arlo Guthrie (1947–)

Arlo Guthrie gave his first public performance at age 13. His career exploded with "Alice's Restaurant" in 1967. An accomplished musician and storyteller, Guthrie is also founder of The Guthrie Center, a not-for-profit interfaith church foundation dedicated to providing a wide range of local and international services. Creator of a program of symphonic arrangements of his own songs and other American classics, *An American Scrapbook*, he has performed the program in over 40 concerts with 27 diferent symphony orchestras. You can learn more about Arlo Guthrie and his music at www.risingsonrecords.net.

Alice Hamilton (1869–1970)

A pioneer in the field of nutrition and founder of occupational medicine, Alice Hamilton was the first woman professor at Harvard Medical School and the first woman to receive the Lasker Award in public health. She received her medical degree from the University of Michigan in 1893. Her discovery of the connection between improper sewage disposal and the role of flies as disease vectors led to reorganization of the Chicago Health Department. She also uncovered the role of noxious chemicals in the health problems of industrial workers. In 1919, Dr. Hamilton became the first woman on the staff of Harvard Medical School. After retiring from Harvard in 1935, she consulted for the Division of Labor Standards of the U.S. Labor Department. In 1943 her autobiography *Exploring the Dangerous Trades* was published. From 1944 to 1949, she was president of the National Consumers League. She spent her last years gardening and painting and died in 1970 a few months after her one hundredth birthday. For more information about Dr. Hamilton, see www.nlm.nih.gov/changingthefaceofmedicine/physicians/biography_137.html.

Joy Harjo

Joy Harjo is a poet, musician, writer, and performer. She has published several books including *How We Became Human: New and Selected Poems*; *A Map to the Next World; Poems* and *Talks*; and *The Woman Who Fell from the Sky*. She is co-editor of an anthology of native women's writing, *Reinventing the Enemy's Language, Native Women's Writing of North America*. She performs internationally as a saxaphone player. Music projects include *Native Joy for Real* (Meiko records). She is a member of the Muscogee Nation, a member of the Talahassee Wakokaye Grounds. She is a professor at UCLA and lives in Honolulu. For more information about Joy Harjo and her work, see www.joyharjo.com.

Lida Gustava Heymann (1868–1943)

Lida Gustava Heymann, the daughter of a wealthy senator, was a founder of the German women's suffrage movement, co-vice president of WILPF, and friend and companion of Anita Augusburg. She established a sewing school for the poor, and used her inheritance to open day-care centers and a restaurant for working women. After Hitler came to power, she lived in exile in Zurich, Switzerland.

Nazim Hikmet (1902–1963)

Nazim Hikmet's first poems were published when he was 17. He was raised in Turkey and attended university in Moscow. He was arrested and served time in jail in Turkey for his leftist acts. He also lived for many years in Russia. He is author of many published books of poetry, including *Things I Didn't Know I Loved*, *The Day before Tomorrow*, and *The Moscow Symphony*. He died in Moscow in 1963. For more information about Nazim Hikmet and his poetry, see www.poets.org/poet.php/ prmPID/285.

Emily Hobhouse (1860–1926)

Emily Hobhouse was born in Cornwall, England. A member of the Liberal Party, she worked for political reform and women's suffrage. She opposed the Boer War and denounced in particular the way poor women and children were treated by the British Army. In 1900 she formed the Relief Fund for South African Women and Children. She opposed England's participation in World War I, and after the war worked to relieve the condition of starving women and children in Europe. For more information about Emily Hobhouse, see http://zar.co.za/emily.htm.

Aletta Jacobs (1854–1929)

Aletta Jacobs was the Netherlands' first woman physician. She worked for better working conditions for shop girls, safe and available contraception, legalization of prostitution (to better the living conditions of the women), and woman's suffrage. Jacobs was one of five women who visited the Netherlands, Great Britain, Germany, Austria, Hungary, Switzerland, Italy, France, and Belgium attempting to persuade heads of state to end World War I.

Coretta Scott King (1927–)

Coretta Scott King was born and raised in Alabama. She earned degrees in music, education, voice, and violin. In 1953, she married Martin Luther King Jr. Active in both the civil rights movement and the peace movement, she has led goodwill missions to many countries and has been a featured speaker at numerous peace and justice rallies. Following her husband's assassination in 1968, Ms. King devoted many years to developing the Martin Luther King, Jr. Center for Nonviolent Social Change. She has received honorary doctorates from over 60 colleges and universities, and is the author of three books. You can learn more about Coretta Scott King's life and work at www.thekingcenter.org/csk/bio.html.

Martin Luther King Jr. (1929–1968)

Martin Luther King Jr. was born in Georgia. He entered Morehouse College at the age of 15 and graduated in 1948 with a degree in sociology. He then went to Crozer

Theological Seminary and earned a Bachelor of Divinity degree in 1951. He received his doctorate from Harvard University in 1955. Dr. King became known nationally for his leadership in the Montgomery bus boycott. In 1957, he founded the Southern Christian Leadership Conference and was its president until his death in 1968. In addition to his service as a pastor at Ebenezer Baptist Church in Atlanta and his civil rights leadership, Dr. King was an outspoken critic of the war in Vietnam. His books include *Stride toward Freedom*, *Why We Can't Wait*, and *The Trumpet of Conscience*. Dr. King was assassinated while in Memphis, Tennessee, helping to lead sanitation workers in their protest against poor wages and working conditions.

Barbara Lee (1946–)

Congresswoman Barbara Lee was first elected to represent California's Ninth Congressional District in 1998. She is the most senior Democratic woman on the House International Relations Committee, where she serves on the Africa Subcommittee and the Western Hemisphere Subcommittee. She also serves on the House Financial Services Committee, and is the co-chair of the Congressional Progressive Caucus, Whip for the Congressional Black Caucus (CBC), and a Senior Democratic Whip. She also serves as chair of the CBC Task Force on Global HIV/AIDS and co-chair of the CBC Haiti Task Force. Congresswoman Lee has sponsored legislation to protect AIDS orphans and led the bipartisan effort to create a $15 billion fund to fight HIV/AIDS, tuberculosis, and malaria. She has been an outspoken critic of the doctrine of preemptive war, and co-sponsored legislation to create a cabinet level Department of Peace. For more on Congresswoman Lee, see www.house.gov/lee/.

Nikki Nojima Louis

Nikki Nojima Louis worked for 15 years as a West Coast theater artist, as actor, playwright, producer, director, and educator. She has received an Artist Trust Fellowship and Seattle Arts Commission Fellowships; playwriting commissions from Seattle's Group Theatre, Museum of History and Industry, Washington State Centennial Commission, and Women's International League for Peace and Freedom; and funding from the National Endowment for the Arts, National and Washington Civil Liberties Public Education Grants, Puffin Foundation, Jane Addams Peace Fund, and the Arts and Humanities Commissions of Washington, Oregon, Idaho, California, Oklahoma, Pennsylvania, and West Virginia. She continues to tour her multicultural oral history projects to colleges and universities throughout the United States. In 2001, Louis received her MFA from the University of Washington's Creative Writing Program, and her thesis won the David Guterson Fiction Award. During 2001–2002, she received scholarships to writers' conferences at Wesleyan and Provincetown's Fine Arts Work Center and fellowships to residencies at Ragdale, Island Institute, Espy Foundation, and Mary Anderson Center for the Arts. She has won the Ursula LeGuin short fiction contest for a story published in *Rosebud*, been nominated by *Indiana Review* for a Pushcart Prize, and twice nominated for *Best New Voices*. She is presently pursuing a PhD in creative writing and Asian American Literature at Florida State University and working on a collection of linked stories.

Wangari Maathai (1940-)

Wangari Muta Maathai was born in Kenya, Africa, in 1940. She was the first woman in Kenya to earn a doctorate degree, and the first woman to chair the Department of Veterinary Anatomy at the University of Nairobi. While serving in the National Council of Women of Kenya, she began the Green Belt Movement, assisting women in planting more than 20 million trees. She was elected to the Kenyan parliament in 2002 and appointed Assistant Minister for Environment, Natural Resources, and Wildlife. She was awarded the Nobel Peace Prize in 2004.

Mairead Corrigan Maguire (1944-)

Mairead Corrigan Maguire founded the Community of the Peace People in 1976 along with Betty Williams and Ciaran McKeown. Maguire was the aunt of three children who were killed when the driver of a getaway car was shot by a soldier. Maguire and Williams earned the Nobel Peace Prize in 1976 for their work to end religious and political violence in Northern Ireland. In 1991, Mairead was married to Jackie Maguire, widower of her sister Anne (who never recovered from the loss of her children and died in January 1980). In addition to three surviving children from the earlier marriage, Mairead and Jackie are parents of John and Luke. Ms. Maguire is recipient of numerous honors and awards, including the Norwegian People's Prize and an honorary doctorate from Yale University. To learn more about Maguire and her work, see her book *The Vision of Peace: Faith and Hope in Northern Ireland* (Orbis Books) or visit www.peacepeople.com.

Catherine Marshall (1880–1962)

Catherine Marshall was parliamentary secretary of the National Union of Women's Suffrage Societies (NUWSS) in England, and played a key role in helping sustain an alliance between the Labour Party and the NUWSS. During the First World War she resigned from her position in the NUWSS because of her support for the peace movement. After 1917 she suffered from periods of ill health but remained active in the Women's International League for Peace and Freedom. She died in 1962. For more information about Catherine Marshall's life and work see www.wcml.org.uk/group/ncf.htm.

Karen MacKay (1952–)

Karen MacKay was born, raised, and educated in West Virginia, where she learned the oral and string music traditions directly from her elders. After receiving an MA in psychology from West Virginia University in 1976, she worked with severely challenged children while maintaining a private teaching practice to preserve the "old" way of learning guitar, banjo, dulcimer, fiddle, and autoharp. In 1982 Karen wrote and recorded the song/album "West Virginia Woman." "If Every Woman" was written in 1984 and was included on Karen's first singer/songwriter album *Annie Oakley Rides Again!* (no longer available). She moved to the Philadelphia area in 1987 to study at the International School of Shiatsu. Since then she has maintained a private practice as a Shiatsu Practitioner/Reike Master and continues a lifetime of grassroots performing as "The West Virginia Woman."

Jan Maher (1946–)

Jan Maher is an educator and writer. She lives in Seattle, Washington, where she teaches theories of learning and human development, curriculum and instruction, and social studies and integrated arts methods in graduate teacher preparation programs. Her plays include *Intruders, Ismene,* and *Widow's Walk.* The latter was a finalist in the Actors Theater of Louisville Ten-Minute Play Contest. She is author of the novel *Heaven, Indiana* and co-author (with husband Douglas Selwyn) of *History in the Present Tense: Engaging Students Through Inquiry and Action.* For more information, see http: //www.janmaher.com.

Betty McIntosh

Betty McIntosh, originally from Scotland, moved to Australia in 1950. There she began to work on issues of discrimination against refugees from eastern and southern Europe. She joined WILPF in the sixties, working against her government's involvement in the Vietnam War and for nuclear disarmamanent. Read more about her life and work in *Women for All Seasons.*

Golda Meir (1898–1978)

Golda Meir was born in Kiev, grew up in Milwaukee, Wisconsin, and emigrated to Israel in 1921. She was active in Zionist politics and was part of the People's Council signing the proclamation establishing the State of Israel. She served Israel as labor minister and foreign minister before becoming prime minister in 1969. She resigned in 1974 in the aftermath of the Yom Kippur War.

Jeanne Melin

A French delegate to the Fourth International Congress in Zurich, Jeanne Melin made a stirring speech against the male politicians at Versailles, urging women everywhere to struggle for a just and peaceful society.

Rigoberta Menchú Tum (1959–)

Rigoberta Menchú Tum was born in Guatemala and raised in the Quiche branch of the Mayan culture. She became involved in social reform activities and the women's rights movement when she was a teenager. In 1979 she joined the Committee of the Peasant Union working for better conditions for farm workers on the Pacific Coast. Her father, mother, and brother were all arrested, tortured, and killed by the military. She wrote her autobiography, *I, Rigoberta Menchú,* while she was living in exile in Mexico. In 1992, she was awarded the Nobel Peace Prize. For more information about her life and work, see: http://nobelprize.org/peace/laureates/1992/tum-bio.html.

Gertrude Mongella (1945–)

Gertrude Mongella was born in Tanzania (then Tanganyika). She earned a degree in education from the University College of Dar-es-Salaam, then entered into public life in 1975 as a member of the East African Legislative Assembly. She has held several ministerial positions, including Minister of State for Women's Affairs, Minister of Lands, Natural Resources and Tourism, and Minister Without Portfolio in the President's Office. She is special advisor to the ECA Executive Secretary and to the UNESCO Director General in the United Nations, and was nominated by the Organization of African Unity Secretary General as a member of the newly formed African Women's Committee for Peace and Development. In 1996, she founded the nongovernmental organization Advocacy for Women in Africa, which is based in Tanzania. To read more about Gertrude Mongella, go to http://www.un.org/womenwatch/news/articles/mongella.htm.

Alva Myrdal (1902–1986)

Alva Myrdal was born in Uppsala, Sweden, in 1902, graduated from university in 1924, and married Gunnar Myrdal the same year. A member of the Social Democrat Party in Sweden, she was appointed to the Government Commission on International Post-War Aid and Reconstruction. In 1949 and 1950 she headed UNO's section dealing with welfare policy, and from 1950 to 1955 she chaired UNESCO's social science section. She was appointed Swedish ambassador to India in 1955. In 1962 she was nominated Sweden's representative to the Geneva disarmament conference and became a member of Parliament. She became a member of the cabinet in 1967, given the special task of promoting disarmament. Myrdal was awarded the Nobel Peace Prize in 1982. She is author of *Dynamics of European Nuclear Disarmament* (Nottingham: Spokesman, 1981) and *The Game of Disarmament: How the United States and Russia Run the Arms Race* (New York: Pantheon, 1982). For more information about Alva Myrdal's life and work, see http://nobelprize.org/peace/laureates/1982/myrdal-bio.html.

Holly Near (1949–)

Holly Near is an entertainer, teacher, and activist. Her professional career began with film and television performances, and an appearance in *Hair* on Broadway. As a songwriter and singer, she has collaborated creatively with such artists as Ronnie Gilbert, Pete Seeger, Arlo Guthrie, Bernice Johnson Reagon, Bonnie Raitt, and Cris Williamson. In 1972, she founded Redwood Records, becoming a major force in alternative music for nearly 20 years. She has received many awards for her work for social change, including honors from the ACLU, the National Lawyer's Guild, the National Organization for Women, and *Ms.* magazine. Near has released over 20 recordings and appeared as a guest on many others. She is also author of an autobiography, *Fire in the Rain: Singer in the Storm* (currently out of print) and a children's book, *The Great Peace March*. Her most recent recording is *Edge*, released on her own label, Calico Tracks Music. You can learn more about Holly Near and her work at www.hollynear.com.

Mildred Scott Olmsted (1890–1990)

Mildred Scott Olmsted, peace activist and suffragist, was born in Pennsylvania in 1890. She graduated with a degree in history from Smith College in 1912. In 1919, she traveled to France where she organized recreation for soldiers through the YMCA and while in Paris met Jane Addams. In 1920, she helped organize the feeding of famine-stricken Bavarian children. After returning to the United States, Olmsted was assistant director of the White-Williams Foundation from 1920 to 1922. She worked for birth control, women's suffrage, civil liberties, animal protection, and conservation. She founded the social work department at Bryn Mawr Hospital. In 1922, Olmsted became executive secretary of the Pennsylvania Branch of the Women's International League for Peace and Freedom (WILPF) and national organization secretary of WILPF, U.S. Section in 1934. In 1946, she became national administrative secretary, holding that position until she retired in 1966. She remained active in WILPF as executive director emerita. For more information about the life and work of Mildred Scott Olmsted, see www.swarthmore.edu/Library/peace/DG051-099/DG082MSOlmsted.html.

Frantiska Plaminkova (1875–1943)

Frantiska Plaminkova was a Czech teacher, feminist, and politician who worked for equal rights for women and campaigned to overturn the so-called celibacy law that limited the rights of teachers and other female state employees. She helped establish many Czech women's associations, including the Czech Women's Club. She later became a senator. She was executed by the Nazis in 1943. For more about Frantiska Plaminkova, see www.ce-review.org/99/14/koenig14the.html.

Mrs. Lowell Putnam

Mrs. Lowell Putnam was sister of A. Lawrence Lowell, president of Harvard University 1956–1943. Mrs. Putnam was instrumental in establishing the Putnam Competition, a national competition in mathematics.

Kathleen Jessie Raine (1908–2003)

Kathleen Raine was a London-born scholar and poet. She was an expert on Blake and Yeats, and shared their visionary tradition, valuing the powers of imagination and nature. She was a founder of the literary magazine *Temenos* and the Temenos Academy, which she characterized as "an association dedicated to the teaching and dissemination of the perennial wisdom, which has been the ground of every civilisation." Raine won several awards, including the Edna St. Vincent Millay Prize from the American Poetry Society and the Queens Gold Medal for Poetry. For more information on Katheen Raine and links to some of her poems, see http://oldpoetry.com/authors/Kathleen%20Raine. For more information about the Temenos Academy, see http://www.temenosacademy.org.

Jeannette Rankin (1880–1973)

Jeannette Rankin was a suffragist, pacifist, and the first woman to be elected to the United States House of Representatives. Born on a ranch in Montana, she worked for suffrage in that state, where women won the vote in 1914 (six years earlier than ratification of the Nineteenth Amendment, giving women the right to vote nationally). Elected on the Republican ticket in 1916, she helped draft the Nineteenth Amendment. Rankin opposed U.S. entry in World War I, and probably as a result of that stand, was not re-elected. She ran again for Congress in 1940, was again elected, and again opposed U.S. entry into a world war, casting the only vote in the House of Representatives against joining World War II. When not holding elective office, Rankin continued to work on peace and women's issues. Ms. Rankin was honored with a statue in Statuary Hall of the U.S. Capitol Building, installed in 1985. For information about the Jeannette Rankin Foundation, see www.rankinfoundation. org. For information about her research papers, see http://bioguide. congress.gov/scripts/guidedisplay.pl?index=R000055.

Theodore Roosevelt (1858–1919)

Theodore Roosevelt gained fame and the name *Rough Rider* as a result of his leadership of a cavalry unit in the Spanish American War, which he wrote about in his book *The Rough Riders*. Elected vice-president, he succeeded to the presidency after President McKinley was assassinated in 1901. In 1904, he was elected to a full term as president. During his presidency, he established the U.S. Forest Service. Roosevelt won the Nobel Peace Prize for his role helping to bring about an end to the war between Japan and Russia. You can read more about his Peace Prize at http://nobelprize.org/peace/laureates/1906/.

Nafis Sadik

Nafis Sadik, a Pakistani national, was born in India. She earned her medical degree from Dow College. Dr. Sadik was executive director of the United Nations Population Fund (UNFPA), with the rank of under-secretary-general, from 1987 through 2000. She was the first woman to head a major UN voluntarily funded program. Dr. Sadik has written numerous articles for leading publications in the family planning, health, and population and development fields, and edited several books, among them: *Population: The UNFPA Experience* (New York University Press, 1984), *Population Policies and Programmes: Lessons Learned from Two Decades of Experience* (New York University Press, 1991), and *Making a Difference: Twenty-five Years of UNFPA Experience* (Banson, London, United Kingdom, 1994). She is a member of the Board of Governors of the Foundation for Human Development and a member of the South Asian Commission on the Asian Challenge. For more information about Dr. Nafis Sadik, see www.un.org/News/dh/hlpanel/sadik-bio.htm.

Pamella Saffer

Pamella Saffer's Assyrian ancestors were from Mesopotamia, the land between the Tigris and Euphrates rivers, but long ago they migrated north to eastern Turkey where they lived with Armenians and Kurds. From there they came to the northeastern United States. Her career has a dual focus in international affairs and arts and culture. She has a special interest in indigenous cultures and women as caretakers of the spiritual traditions of ancient cultures.

Rosika Schwimmer (1877–1948)

Rosika Schwimmer worked as a bookkeeper as a young woman, helped to establish the National Association of Women Office Workers in Austria-Hungary, and served as its president between 1897 and 1912. She was an active campaigner for women's suffrage in Austria-Hungary, and served as corresponding secretary of the International Woman Suffrage Alliance. In 1914, Schwimmer traveled to the United States to meet with President Woodrow Wilson and Secretary of State William Jennings Bryan, urging them to try to bring the war to an end. She helped found the Woman's Peace Party, and was a delegate to the First International Congress at The Hague. She became vice-president of WILPF, and after the Armistice became Hungary's ambassador to Switzerland. When the fascists came to power, she left Hungary and eventually emigrated to the United States, where she worked to help create a World Centre for Women's Archives. (The motto for the archive was "No documents, no history.") The venture ended in 1940 due to lack of funds. Rosika Schwimmer died in New York in 1948. For more information about her, see www.swarthmore.edu/Library/peace/CDGA.S-Z/schwimmer.htm.

Cindy Sheehan (1957-   )

Cindy Sheehan became an antiwar activist after her son Casey was killed in an ambush in Iraq in 2004. In August 2005 she established Camp Casey, a peace encampment named in his honor, near President Bush's home in Crawford, Texas. She is a founder of Gold Star Families for Peace and author of *Not One More Mother's Child* (KOA Books, 2005). You can read more about Cindy Sheehan and her efforts to bring the troops back from Iraq at a number of websites, including http://www.meetwithcindy.org/ and www.angelfire.com/sk3/spkhntrca/Casey.html.

Mary Sheepshanks (1872–1958)

Mary Sheepshanks was born in Liverpool, graduated from Newnham College, Cambridge, and began a career in social work. She was active in the women's suffrage movement, eventually becoming secretary of the International Woman Suffrage Association in London. She opposed World War I, but organized aid for Belgian refugees and German women stranded in England. She was unable to attend the First International Conference at The Hague due to the closure of the North Sea shipping lanes. After the war ended, she was secretary of the Fight the Famine Council, and in 1927 became international secretary of WILPF. During the 1930s, she organized relief for child victims of the Spanish Civil War. During World War II, she renounced pacifism in the face of the Nazi threat. She died in 1958. For more about Mary Sheepshanks, see www.archiveshub.ac.uk/news/0409ms.html.

Mavis Smallberg

Mavis Smallberg is a South African poet, performer, and educator. She has written and performed her poetry since the early 1980s, and has been part of several cultural collectives, all of which exist to educate, inspire, encourage, and promote writing and arts and culture in general. Her work has been published in several national and international anthologies of which the latest are: *A Gift of African Thoughts*, a publication to celebrate Thabo Mbeki's inauguration as state president in 2000, *Women on War: An International Anthology of Writing from Antiquity to the Present* (Daniela Gioseffi, Ed., Feminist Press at the City University of New York, 2003), *Women Writing Africa*, (Wits University Press, Johannesburg, 2003) and *Imagination in a Troubled Space: A SA Poetry Reader* (Michaela Borzorg & Prof. Dorothea Steiner, Ed., University of Salzburg, Austria). Ms. Smallberg is a core member of WEAVE (Women's Education and Artistic Voice Expression), a black women's writing and publishing collective in Capetown, South Africa. She currently works at the Robben Island Museum.

Aung San Suu Kyi (1945–)

Aung San Suu Kyi was born in Rangoon, Burma, the daughter of a commander in the Burma Independence Army who was assassinated when she was 2 years old. In 1960 her mother was appointed Burma's ambassador to India, where Suu Kyi attended high school and college. She went on to earn a BA at Oxford University, where she met her husband Michael Aris. They had two sons. She returned to Burma in 1988 to be with her terminally ill mother, and subsequently became involved in the burgeoning democratic movement. When the party she headed won elections, the results were ignored, and Suu Kyi, along with many others, was placed under house arrest. She was granted the Nobel Peace Prize for her work in 1991. The film *Beyond Rangoon* is based on her life. For more about Aung San Suu Kyi and her work, see www.dassk.com/.

Joan Szymko

Joan Szymko has 20 years of experience as a choral conductor, composer, teacher, and performer in the Pacific Northwest. She led the Seattle Women's Ensemble for 10 years and joined the Concord Community of Choirs of Portland, Oregon, in the fall of 1993, becoming the director of the 100-plus voices of Aurora Chorus—women in harmony for peace. Szymko formed Viriditas, a select women's chamber ensemble in 1994. Viriditas is featured on Szymko's 1998 CD recording of her compositions, *Openings*. Szymko's compositions and arrangements have been performed by choruses across the country. Her published scores have been included in workshops and reading sessions presented by Rodney Eichenberger, René Clausen, Andre Thomas, Patricia Hennings, and at national and regional ACDA (American Choral Directors Association) conventions. Her choral music is published by Santa Barbara Music Publishing and Treble Clef Music Press. For more about Joan Szymko and her work, see www.szymko.com.

Gail Tremblay (1945–)

Gail Tremblay was born in Buffalo, New York, of Onondaga/Micmac and French Canadian ancestry. In addition to her poetry, she is a widely exhibited visual artist. *Indian Signing*, Revised Edition (Calyx Books 1998) includes many black and white plates of her work. She is on the faculty of the Evergreen State College in Olympia, Washington. Her other published works include *Close to Home* (University of Nebraska, 1981), and *Night Gives Women the World* (Omaha Printing Company, 1979).

Alice Walker (1944–)

Alice Walker was born in Georgia and graduated from Sarah Lawrence College in 1965. Her first book of poems was published in 1968, her first novel in 1970. Walker won the Pulitzer Prize for her novel *The Color Purple*. Other novels include *Meridian, The Temple of My Familiar, Possessing the Secret of Joy,* and *By the Light of My Father's Smile: A Novel.* Many of her essays are included in *In Search of Our Mothers' Gardens.* She has been an active campaigner for economic justice, conservation, human rights and women's rights in particular, including writing and raising attention to the practice of female genital mutilation.

Jody Williams (1950–)

Jody Williams is the founding coordinator of the International Committee to Ban Landmines (ICBL), and oversaw its growth from a membership of 6 non-governmental organizations (NGOs) in 1992 to more than 1,300 NGOs in over 85 countries today. An international organizer and activist, teacher, and writer, Williams has served since February 1998 as a campaign ambassador for ICBL, speaking on its behalf all over the world. Ms. Williams is also a Distinguished Visiting Professor of Social Work and Global Justice in the Graduate School of Social Work at the University of Houston. Prior to beginning the ICBL, Williams coordinated aid and education projects building public awareness about U.S. policy toward Central America. In 1997, Williams and the ICBL were awarded the Nobel Peace Prize. You can read more about Jody Williams and the ICBL at www.icbl.org.

Anne Wiltsher (1951–2004)

Anne Wiltsher was born in Exeter, grew up in Devon, and moved to London when she was 18 to pursue a career in journalism. She wrote for a number of magazines as well as freelancing for *The Guardian* and *The Independent.* She was active in the National Union of Journalists, Women's Movement, and the Campaign for Nuclear Disarmament at Greenham Common. Her book *Most Dangerous Women* was adapted by the BBC television history program *Timewatch.* In 1982 she met Peter Ludbrook, her partner for the rest of her life. Their daughter was born in 1987. She returned to journalism, and in her last years was deputy features editor for *Nursery World.* In August 2003 she was overwhelmed by a depressive breakdown that was unresponsive to treatment, and in February 2004 took her own life.

Virginia Woolf (1882–1941)

Virginia Woolf was a feminist, socialist, and pacifist, and a major British novelist, essayist, and critic, one of the leaders in the literary movement of modernism. Her work is characterized by the technique known as stream of consciousness. Her novels include *To the Lighthouse* and *Mrs. Dalloway,* the latter being the inspiration for the novel and film *The Hours.* In 1904, Woolf, her sister Vanessa, and two brothers moved to the house in Bloomsbury that became the center of the Bloomsbury Group. She married Leonard Woolf in 1912. Woolf was a prolific essayist as well as a novelist. In *Three Guineas,* she looked at the necessity for women to claim their own history and literature. Woolf drowned herself in 1941. For more about Virginia Woolf's work, see the website of the Virginia Woolf Society at http://orlando.jp.org/VWSGB/.

Appendix B

Peace and Justice Organizations

L isted below are but a few of the peace and justice organizations that have formed in response to the crisis of armed warfare in the world. Each has its own particular focus, its own particular point of origin. Organizational descriptions are taken from each group's website.

The Carter Center   www.cartercenter.org

The Carter Center, in partnership with Emory University, is committed to advancing human rights and alleviating unnecessary human suffering. Founded in 1982 by former U.S. President Jimmy Carter and his wife, Rosalynn, the Atlanta-based Center has helped to improve the quality of life for people in more than 65 countries.

CODEPINK   www.codepink4peace.org

CODEPINK is a women-initiated grassroots peace and social justice movement that seeks positive social change through proactive, creative protest and nonviolent direct action.

Educators for Social Responsibility   www.esrnational.org

Educators for Social Responsibility (ESR) helps educators create safe, caring, respectful, and productive learning environments. We also help educators work with young people to develop the social skills, emotional competencies, and qualities of character they need to succeed in school and become contributing members of their communities.

Fellowship of Reconciliation International   www.ifor.org (United States branch www.forusa.org)

The International Fellowship of Reconciliation (IFOR) is an international spiritually based movement composed of people who commit themselves to active nonviolence as a way of life and as a means of transformation—personal, social, economic, and political. IFOR has operational relations status with the United Nations (UNESCO).

The Fellowship of Reconciliation envisions a world of justice, peace, and freedom. It is a revolutionary vision of a beloved community where differences are respected, conflicts addressed nonviolently, oppressive structures dismantled, and where people live in harmony with the earth. The Fellowship of Reconciliation seeks to replace violence, war, racism, and economic injustice with nonviolence, peace, and justice. We are an interfaith organization committed to active nonviolence as a transforming way of life and as a means of radical change. We educate, train, build coalitions, and engage in nonviolent and compassionate actions locally, nationally, and globally.

Global Women's Strike   www.globalwomenstrike.net

The Global Women's Strike was born in 1999, when women in Ireland decided to welcome the new millennium with a national general strike. They asked the International Wages for Housework Campaign to support their call, and we called on women all over the world to make the Strike global on 8 March 2000. The Strike came out of a long grassroots history, starting in 1952 with a little pamphlet called *A Woman's Place* and continuing with *Power of Women and the Subversion of the Community*, now a classic, in 1972, and *Sex, Race and Class* in 1973. All three made the case that the work women do for wages is a second job, that the work we do in the home and in the community without wages, producing all the workers of the world, and our struggle to change the world, were invisible but central. Since then, we have been campaigning to get RECOGNITION and WAGES for all the unwaged work women do, as well as for PAY EQUITY—these are JOINT LEVERS against women's poverty, exploitation, and discrimination of every kind. According to the UN, women do two thirds of the world's work: from breastfeeding and raising children to caring for those who are sick, older, or disabled, to growing, preparing, and cooking the food that feeds families, communities, and continents (80 percent of food consumed in Africa is grown by women), to volunteer work and to work in the informal economy as cleaners, seamstresses, street sellers, sex workers, as well as work in the formal economy. Here again women's work is often caring for people, in hospitals and schools, as domestic workers, childminders, personal assistants . . . or in sweatshops—jobs where men who do comparable work also get low pay. But women get the lowest, and often face sexual and racial harassment.

Gold Star Families for Peace   www.gsfp.org

Gold Star Families for Peace was founded by families of soldiers who have died as a result of war (primarily, but not limited to the invasion/occupation of Iraq). Their mission is to organize to be a positive force in our world to bring our country's sons and daughters home from Iraq, to minimize the "human cost" of this war, and to prevent other families from experiencing the pain they are feeling as the result of their losses. They also hope to be lifetime support for each other. Anyone who has had a relative killed as a result of war can join. There is a specific emphasis on those who lost relatives in the invasion/occupation of Iraq.

Peace Action www.peace-action.org

Peace Action, the merger of SANE and The Freeze, has effectively mobilized for peace and disarmament for over forty years. As the nation's largest grassroots peace group we get results: from the 1963 treaty to ban above ground nuclear testing, to the 1996 signing of the Comprehensive Test Ban Treaty, from ending the war in Vietnam, to blocking weapons sales to human rights abusing countries. We are proof that ordinary people can change the world.

Peaceful Tomorrows www.peacefultomorrows.org

Peaceful Tomorrows is an organization founded by family members of those killed on September 11th who have united to turn our grief into action for peace. By developing and advocating nonviolent options and actions in the pursuit of justice, we hope to break the cycles of violence engendered by war and terrorism. Acknowledging our common experience with all people affected by violence throughout the world, we work to create a safer and more peaceful world for everyone.

Physicians for Social Responsibility www.psr.org

Physicians for Social Responsibility is committed to the elimination of nuclear and other weapons of mass destruction, the achievement of a sustainable environment, and the reduction of violence and its causes. Physicians for Social Responsibility (PSR) is a leading public policy organization with 24,000 members representing the medical and public health professions and concerned citizens, working together for nuclear disarmament, a healthful environment, and an end to the epidemic of gun violence.

Ploughshares www.ploughshares.org

The Ploughshares Fund is a public grantmaking foundation that supports initiatives to prevent the spread and use of nuclear, biological, and chemical weapons and other weapons of war, and to prevent conflicts that could lead to the use of weapons of mass destruction.

Veterans For Peace www.veteransforpeace.org/

Veterans For Peace is a national organization founded in 1985. It is structured around a national office in Saint Louis, MO, and comprised of members across the country organized in chapters or as at-large members. There is an annual convention in August for members from across the nation. Members receive periodic VFP publications.

The organization includes men and women veterans from World War II, Korea, Vietnam, the Gulf War, and other conflicts as well as peacetime veterans. Our collective experience tells us wars are easy to start and hard to stop and that those hurt are often the innocent. Thus, other means of problem solving are necessary.

Veterans For Peace is an official non-governmental organization (NGO) represented at the UN.

Voices in the Wilderness   http://vitw.org

Voices in the Wilderness (VitW) was formed in 1996 to nonviolently challenge the economic warfare being waged by the US against the people of Iraq. Voices continues its work today, acting to end the US occupation of Iraq.

Volunteers for Peace   www.vfp.org

VFP is a Vermont non-profit 501 (c) (3) membership corporation that has been co-ordinating International Voluntary Service since 1982. They do not have any religious or political affiliation. VFP is an Executive Committee member of the Coordinating Committee for International Voluntary Service (CCIVS) at UNESCO and works in cooperation with Service Civil International (SCI), the Alliance of European Voluntary Service Organizations, and International Youth Action for Peace (YAP). The history of International Voluntary Service dates back more than 80 years. The VFP office staff, Advisory Board, and thousands of volunteers in the field help facilitate this program. Within the CCIVS network, over 100,000 volunteers are exchanged annually. In 2004, VFP exchanged over 1,200 volunteers.

War Resisters League   www.warresisters.org

Believing war to be a crime against humanity, the War Resisters League, founded in 1923, advocates Gandhian nonviolence as the method for creating a democratic society free of war, racism, sexism, and human exploitation.

Women's International League for Peace and Freedom   www.wilpf.org

WILPF envisions a transformed world at peace, where there is racial, social, and economic justice for all people everywhere—a world in which the needs of all people are met in a fair and equitable manner, all people equally participate in making the decisions that affect them, the interconnected web of life is acknowledged and celebrated in diverse ways and communities, and human societies are designed and organized for sustainable existence. WILPF members create the peaceful transformation they wish to see in the world by making connections that provide continuity with the past so that knowledge of historical events and patterns informs current activities for change, create analysis and action that reflect and reinforce each other; link and challenge root causes of oppression, especially racism, sexism, heterosexism, militarism, economic disparity, and political disempowerment; and build and strengthen relationships and movements for justice, peace, and radical democracy.

A Few Highlights from WILPF's First Ninety Years:

1915   The Hague Congress: women demand an end to WWI

1919   The Zurich Conference: WILPF denounces the Treaty of Versailles as creating the conditions for future war

1924   Scientists mobilized to refuse to participate in war research

1926   Mission to Haiti investigates effects of U.S. Marine occupation

1931   Founding member Jane Addams is first American woman to win Nobel Peace Prize

1945   WILPF is a founding non-governmental organization (NGO) at the first United Nations Conference in San Francisco

1946   WILPF founding member Emily Green Balch wins Nobel Peace Prize

1969   WILPF sponsors an international conference to end chemical and biological warfare

1971   WILPF signs Women's Peace Treaty in Vietnam

1973   WILPF sends mission to Chile to investigate human rights violations

1975   WILPF convenes Women's Disarmament Conference at the UN in New York

1984   WILPF launches a worldwide campaign for the Comprehensive Test Ban Treaty

1990   WILPF launches a worldwide Women vs. Violence campaign

1994   WILPF launches the Practice Anti-Racism Campaign

1997   WILPF hosts Symposium on Truth and Reconciliation

1998   Legislative Office opened; WILPF re-establishes a presence in Washington, D.C.

2005   WILPF launches Save the Water Campaign

Appendix C

Nobel Peace Prize Winners

For more information about the Nobel Peace Prize and prize winners, see http://nobelprize.org/peace/laureates.

2005　Mohamed Elbaradei and the International Atomic Energy Agency of the United Nations

2004　Wangari Maathai

2003　Shirin Ebadi

2002　Jimmy Carter

2001　United Nations and Kofi Annan

2000　Kim Dae-jung

1999　Médecins Sans Frontières

1998　John Hume and David Trimble

1997　International Campaign to Ban Landmines and Jody Williams

1996　Carlos Filipe Ximenes Belo and José Ramos-Horta

1995　Joseph Rotblat and Pugwash Conferences on Science and World Affairs

1994　Yasser Arafat, Shimon Peres, and Yitzhak Rabin

1993　Nelson Mandela and F.W. de Klerk

1992　Rigoberta Menchú Tum

1991　Aung San Suu Kyi

1990　Mikhail Gorbachev

1989　The 14th Dalai Lama

1988　United Nations Peacekeeping Forces

1987　Oscar Arias Sánchez

1986   Elie Wiesel

1985   International Physicians for the Prevention of Nuclear War

1984   Desmond Tutu

1983   Lech Walesa

1982   Alva Myrdal and Alfonso García Robles

1981   Office of the United Nations High Commissioner for Refugees

1980   Adolfo Pérez Esquivel

1979   Mother Teresa

1978   Anwar al-Sadat and Menachem Begin

1977   Amnesty International

1976   Betty Williams and Mairead Corrigan

1975   Andrei Sakharov

1974   Seán MacBride and Eisaku Sato

1973   Henry Kissinger and Le Duc Tho

1972   The prize money for 1972 was allocated to the Main Fund

1971   Willy Brandt

1970   Norman Borlaug

1969   International Labour Organization

1968   René Cassin

1967   The prize money was allocated one-third piece to the Main Fund and two-thirds piece to the Special Fund of this prize section

1966   The prize money was allocated to the Special Fund of this prize section

1965   United Nations Children's Fund

1964   Martin Luther King Jr.

1963   International Committee of the Red Cross and League of Red Cross Societies

1962   Linus Pauling

1961   Dag Hammarskjöld

1960   Albert Lutuli

1959   Philip Noel-Baker

1958   Georges Pire

1957   Lester Bowles Pearson

1956   The prize money was allocated one-third piece to the Main Fund and two-thirds piece to the Special Fund of this prize section

1955   The prize money was allocated to the Special Fund of this prize section

1954   Office of the United Nations High Commissioner for Refugees

1953   George C. Marshall

1952   Albert Schweitzer

1951   Léon Jouhaux

1950   Ralph Bunche

1949   Lord Boyd Orr

1948   The prize money was allocated one-third piece to the Main Fund and two-thirds piece to the Special Fund of this prize section

1947   Friends Service Council and American Friends Service Committee

1946   Emily Greene Balch and John R. Mott

1945   Cordell Hull

1944   International Committee of the Red Cross

1943   The prize money was allocated one-third piece to the Main Fund and two-thirds piece to the Special Fund of this prize section

1942   The prize money was allocated one-third piece to the Main Fund and two-thirds piece to the Special Fund of this prize section

1941   The prize money was allocated one-third piece to the Main Fund and two-thirds piece to the Special Fund of this prize section

1940   The prize money was allocated one-third piece to the Main Fund and two-thirds piece to the Special Fund of this prize section

1939   The prize money was allocated one-third piece to the Main Fund and two-thirds piece to the Special Fund of this prize section

1938   Nansen International Office for Refugees

1937   Robert Cecil

1936   Carlos Saavedra Lamas

1935   Carl von Ossietzky

1934   Arthur Henderson

1933   Sir Norman Angell

1932   The prize money was allocated to the Special Fund of this prize section

1931   Jane Addams and Nicholas Murray Butler

1930   Nathan Söderblom

1929   Frank B. Kellogg

1928   The prize money was allocated to the Special Fund of this prize section

1927   Ferdinand Buisson and Ludwig Quidde

1926   Aristide Briand and Gustav Stresemann

1925   Sir Austen Chamberlain and Charles G. Dawes

1924   The prize money was allocated to the Special Fund of this prize section

1923   The prize money was allocated to the Special Fund of this prize section

1922	Fridtjof Nansen
1921	Hjalmar Branting and Christian Lange
1920	Léon Bourgeois
1919	Woodrow Wilson
1918	The prize money was allocated to the Special Fund of this prize section
1917	International Committee of the Red Cross
1916	The prize money was allocated to the Special Fund of this prize section
1915	The prize money was allocated to the Special Fund of this prize section
1914	The prize money was allocated to the Special Fund of this prize section
1913	Henri La Fontaine
1912	Elihu Root
1911	Tobias Asser and Alfred Fried
1910	Permanent International Peace Bureau
1909	Auguste Beernaert and Paul Henri d'Estournelles de Constant
1908	Klas Pontus Arnoldson and Fredrik Bajer
1907	Ernesto Teodoro Moneta and Louis Renault
1906	Theodore Roosevelt
1905	Bertha von Suttner
1904	Institute of International Law
1903	Randal Cremer
1902	Élie Ducommun and Albert Gobat
1901	Henry Dunant and Frédéric Passy

Appendix D

Teaching Peace—A Sample Bibliography

Thanks to the Internet, it isn't difficult to find resources for teaching about peace and social justice issues. Below are just a few of the resources you can access online. Definitions and mission statements are taken from the organizations' material.

Rethinking Schools   www.rethinkingschools.org

Rethinking Schools is firmly committed to equity and to the vision that public education is central to the creation of a humane, caring, multiracial democracy.

Teaching Tolerance   www.tolerance.org

Founded in 1991 by the Southern Poverty Law Center, Teaching Tolerance provides educators with free educational materials that promote respect for differences and appreciation of diversity in the classroom and beyond.

The United Nations Cyber Schoolbus   www.un.org/cyberschoolbus/peace/index.asp

The United Nations Cyber Schoolbus was created in 1996 as the online education component of the Global Teaching and Learning Project, whose mission is to promote education about international issues and the United Nations.

Wells, Leah C. (2003) *Teaching Peace: A Guide for the Classroom and Everyday Life.* Nuclear Age Peace Foundation, retrievable online at   www.wagingpeace. org/menu/ programs/ youth-outreach/peace-ed-book/teaching-peace.pdf

For bibliographies of books related to teaching peace, consult the websites of individual peace and social justice organizations. Many of them include links to recommended lists, often with the option to purchase the books through the organization website.

Appendix E

Working with Primary Sources

The following pages are worksheets for analysis of various sorts of primary source documents. These worksheets are adapted and used with permission from those developed by National Archives and Records Administration, located on the Internet at www.archives.gov/digital_classroom/lessons/analysis_ worksheets/worksheets.html.

Written Document Analysis Worksheet

1. **Type of Document** (check one)

   ___ Speech   ___ Memorandum   ___ Press Release
   ___ Letter   ___ Journal   ___ Contract
   ___ Treaty   ___ Birth Certificate   ___ Death Certificate
   ___ Poem   ___ Other (Give details):

2. **Unique Physical Qualities of the Document:**

   ___ Interesting letterhead   ___ Handwritten   ___ Typed
   ___ Seals   ___ Notations   ___ "Received" Stamp
   ___ Other (describe)

3. **Date(s) of Document:**

4. **Author or Creator of the Document:**

Position (Title):

5. **For what audience was the document written?**

6. **Document Information** (There are many possible ways to answer A–E.)

   A. List three things the author said that you think are important:

       1.

       2.

       3.

   B. Why do you think this document was written?

   C. What evidence in the document helps you know why it was written? Quote from the document.

   D. List two things the document tells you about life in the United States or the world at the time it was written:

       1.

       2.

   E. Write a question to the author that is left unanswered by the document:

Adapted from materials designed and developed by the Education Staff, National Archives and Records Administration, Washington, DC 20408.

Page URL: www.archives.gov/digital_classroom/lessons/analysis_worksheets/worksheets.html.

Sound Recording Analysis Worksheet

1. **Pre-listening**
   A. Whose voices will you hear on this recording?
   B. What is the date of this recording?
   C. Where was this recording made?

2. **Listening**
   A. Type of sound recording (check one):
   ___ Policy speech   ___ Congressional testimony   ___ News report
   ___ Interview   ___ Entertainment broadcast   ___ Press conference
   ___ Convention proceedings   ___ Campaign speech
   ___ Arguments before a court   ___ Panel discussion
   ___ Other (Give details):

   B. Unique physical qualities of the recording:
   ___ Music   ___ Live broadcast   ___ Narrated
   ___ Special sound effects   ___ Background sound

   C. What is the tone or mood of this recording?

3. **Post-listening (or repeated listening)**
   A. List three things in this sound recording that you think are important:
      1.
      2.
      3.

   B. Why do you think the original broadcast was made and for what audience?

   C. What evidence in the recording helps you to know why it was made?

   D. List two things this sound recording tells you about life in the United States at the time it was made:
      1.
      2.

   E. Write a question to the broadcaster that is left unanswered by this sound recording.

   F. What information do you gain about this event that would not be conveyed by a written transcript? Be specific.

Adapted from materials designed and developed by the Education Staff, National Archives and Records Administration, Washington, DC 20408.

Page URL: www.archives.gov/digital_classroom/lessons/analysis_worksheets/worksheets.html.

Song Lyrics Analysis Worksheet

1. Title of the song:

2. Lyricist and composer:

3. Date or era song was first written or recorded:

4. For what audience was the song composed?

5. List three to five things the songwriter says that you think are important:
    A.
    B.
    C.
    D.
    E.

6. Why do you think this song was written?

7. What evidence in the lyrics helps you know why it was written? Quote from the document.

8. List two things the document tells you about life in the United States or the world at the time it was written:
    A.
    B.

9. What question(s) do you have about this song that you could research further?

Adapted from materials designed and developed by the Education Staff, National Archives and Records Administration, Washington, DC 20408.

Page URL: www.archives.gov/digital_classroom/lessons/analysis_worksheets/worksheets.html.

Photograph Analysis Worksheet

1. Observation

A. Study the photograph for 2 minutes. Form an overall impression of the photograph and then examine individual items. Next, divide the photo into quadrants and study each section to see what new details become visible.

B. Use the chart below to list people, objects, and activities in the photograph.

People	Objects	Activities

2. Inference

Based on what you have observed above, list three things you might infer from this photograph:

A.

B.

C.

3. Questions

A. What questions does this photograph raise in your mind?

B. Where could you find answers to them?

Adapted from materials designed and developed by the Education Staff, National Archives and Records Administration, Washington, DC 20408.

www.archives.gov/digital_classroom/lessons/analysis_worksheets/worksheets.html.

Film or Video Analysis Worksheet

1. **Pre-viewing**
   A. Title of film or video: _____

   Producer:

   B. What do you think you will see in this film or video? List three concepts or ideas that you might expect to see based on the title. List some people you might expect to see based on the title of the film.

   1. Concepts/Ideas:

      a. _____

      b. _____

      c. _____

   2. People:

      a. _____

      b. _____

      c. _____

2. **Viewing**
   A. Type of film or video (check where applicable):

   ___ Animated cartoon   ___ Documentary film   ___ Newsreel
   ___ Propaganda film   ___ Theatrical short subject ___ Training film
   ___ Combat film   ___ Other (describe)

   B. Physical qualities of the film or video (check where applicable):

   ___ Music   ___ Narration   ___ Special effects
   ___ Color   ___ Live action   ___ Background noise
   ___ Animation   ___ Dramatizations

   C. Note how camera angles, lighting, music, narration, and/or editing contribute to creating an atmosphere in this film. What is the mood or tone of the film?

3. **Post-viewing** (or repeated viewing)
   A. What were things that you listed in the previewing activity that were validated by your viewing of the file?

   B. What is the central message(s) of this film?

C. Consider the effectiveness of the film in communicating its message. As a tool of communication, what are its strengths and weaknesses?

D. How do you think the filmmakers wanted the audience to respond?

E. Does this film appeal to the viewer's reason or emotion? How does it make you feel?

F. List two things this motion picture tells you about life in the United States or the world at the time it was made:

1.

2.

G. Write a question to the filmmaker that is left unanswered by the motion picture.

H. What information do you gain about this event that would not be conveyed by a written source? Be specific.

Adapted from materials developed by Education Staff, National Archives and Records Administration, Washington, DC 20408.

URL page: www.archives.gov/digital_classroom/lessons/analysis_worksheets/worksheets.html.

Appendix F

Additional Resource Information

Four anthologies with stories, essays, memoirs, songs, and poems including several used in *Most Dangerous Women:*

My Country is the Whole World: An Anthology of Women's Work on Peace and War published by Cambridge Women's Peace Collective; Pandora Press, 1984.

The Impossible Will Take a Little While: A Citizen's Guide to Hope in a Time of Fear, ed. Paul Rogat Loeb; Basic Books, 2004.

Rise Up Singing : The Group Singing Songbook, Sing Out Publications, 2004

Women on War: An International Anthology of Writings from Antiquity to the Present, ed. Daniela Gioseffi; New York: The Feminist Press 2003

For general background information about the Women's International League for Peace and Freedom:

Most Dangerous Women: Feminist Peace Campaigners of the Great War, by Anne Wiltsher; London, Boston: Pandora Press, 1985

No Peace Without Freedom: Race and the Women's International League for Peace and Freedom, 1915–1975 by Joyce Blackwell; Carbondale: Southern Illinois University Press, 2004

Pioneers for Peace: Women's International League for Peace and Freedom 1915-1965, by Gertrude Bussey and Margaret Tims; London: British Section

Reconstructing Women's Thoughts: The Women's International League for Peace and Freedom Before World War II, by Linda K. Schott; Palo Alto: Stanford University Press, 1997

Women for All Seasons: The Story of the Women's International League for Peace and Freedom, by Catherine Foster; Athens and London: The University of Georgia Press, 1989

A few biographies of WILPF members:

Citizen: Jane Addams and the Struggle for Democracy, by Louise W. Knight; Chicago: University of Chicago Press, 2005

First Lady in Congress: Jeannette Rankin: A Biography, by Hannah Josephson; Indianapolis and New York: Bobbs-Merrill, 1974

One Woman's Passion for Peace and Freedom: The Life of Mildred Scott Olmsted, by Margaret Hope Bacon; Syracuse: Syracuse University Press, 1993

For sheet music and script updates:

Please contact Local Access, c/o Dog Hollow Press, P. O. Box 22287, Seattle, WA 98122-0287, telephone (206) 568-1195.

To learn more about specific songs and monologues in the play *Most Dangerous Women:*

You can retrieve an audio of *Johnny I Hardly Knew Ya'* with slightly different lyrics than those used in *Most Dangerous Women*, at http://www.chivalry.com/cantaria/lyrics/johnnyihardlyknewye.html.

Jane Addams reporting on the First Congress at the Hague—full text can be found in the *New York Times*, April 29, 1915, p2.

I Didn't Raise My Son to be a Soldier - by Paige Wheeler, lyrics adapted from Alfred Bryan. The original lyrics and melody (not the melody composed by Paige Wheeler and used in performances of *Most Dangerous Women*) are retrievable in audio format at http://historymatters.gmu.edu/d/4942.

"Mildred Scott Olmsted Recalls"—the full text of the interview can be found in *Women for All Seasons, op cit.*

Die Gedanken Sind Frei—Song: German traditional, English lyrics by Arthur Kevess © 1950 (renewed) by APPLESEED MUSIC. All rights reserved. This song is widely recorded, including on *Martha Schlamme at the Gate of Horn*, Vanguard VRS-9091 (1961). An audio of the melody and lyrics in German and French are retrievable at http://ingeb.org/Lieder/diegedan.html.

Toyomi Hashimoto Remembers Nagasaki—from *Hellish Years After Hellish Days*, in *Cries for Peace: Experiences of Japanese Victims of World War II*, compiled by the Youth Division of Soka Gakkai; Tokyo: the Japan Times, Ltd. Used by permission. Fuller excerpt reprinted in *Women on War, op cit.*

I Come and Stand at Every Door—Words by Nazim Hikmet, English version by J. Turner. Music by James Waters. © 1961 (renewed) by STORMKING MUSIC, INC. All rights reserved. Used by permission. Recorded on The Byrds, *Fifth Dimension*, original recording remastered; Sony #64847. Audio sample link on product page at www.amazon.com.

If Every Woman—words & music by Karen MacKay, the West Virginia Woman © 1984. Used by permission. Recorded on *Annie Oakley Rides Again* (out of print).

The Ten Commandments on Vietnam—Dr. Martin Luther King Jr., original news coverage in the *New York Times,* "Mrs. King Reads War Decalogue," April 28, 1968, page 73, 1.

Spell Against Sorrow—adapted from poem by Kathleen Raine, printed in *Selected Poems* by Kathleen Raine, distributed in U.S. by Harper and Row (1988).

Dear Son—excerpted from *Dear Luke* by Mairead Corrigan Maguire, used by permission of the author. Fuller text reprinted in *Women on War, op cit.*

As A Woman—lyrics adapted by Joan Szymko from Virginia Woolf *Three Guineas,* fuller text reprinted in *Women on War, op cit.*

The South African Bureau of Information Notes: The Situation in Soweto is Not Abnormal—Mavis Smallberg. Reprinted in *Women on War, op cit.,* titled *Quote from the Bureau of Information, from the* Argus, *August 27, 1986;* "The Situation in Soweto is not Abnormal."

Siph'a mandla Nkosi—An audio is available at www.stationen.fi/juke boxen/jukebox-44-5697.html. Click on the "Lyssna" link. The lyrics are in Zulu and Swedish. *Siph'a mandla Nkosi* is one of thousands of songs sung to uplift people and encourage their hopes when they were being killed or jailed during the struggle to end apartheid in South Africa. Some activists, including Nelson Mandela, spent decades enduring brutal conditions at the Robben Island prison; now, with the end of apartheid, Robben Island is a museum celebrating the triumph of the human spirit over enormous hardship and adversity. For more information on the Robben Island Museum, visit their website at www.robben -island.org.za.

"The right to die of old age" is quoted from Alice Walker's *Living by the Word,* Harvest Books, 1989.

The Women's Party for Survival—Helen Caldicott. Fuller version reprinted in *Women on War, op cit.*

Fresh Peaches—Alice Walker, from *"Only Justice Can Stop a Curse,"* in *In Search of Our Mothers' Gardens* by Alice Walker, published 1984 by Harcourt, Brace, Jovanovich, fuller excerpt reprinted *in Women on War, op cit.* and *The Impossible Will Take a Little While, op cit.*

No More Genocide—Music and lyrics by Holly Near, recorded on *And Still We Sing: The Outspoken Collection,* CD, Calico Tracks Music, 2002, audio sample link on product page at www.amazon.com.

"Zlata Filipovic writes in her diary" excerpted from Zlata's Diary: A Child's Life in Sarajevo, by Zlata Filopovic; Penguin, 1995.

The "Discovery" of America—Joy Harjo. From an interview by Roxanne Dunbar-Ortiz in the newsletter *Crossroads,* reprinted in *Pacific Vision* June 1991 and *Peace and Freedom,* January/February 1992.

Landmines—Jody Williams. The full text can be retrieved at http://nobel prize.org/peace/laureates/1997/williams-lecture.html.

Children of Abraham—Arlo Guthrie. Recorded on *Arlo Guthrie*, Rising Son Records, remastered CD 2005.

Barbara Lee Votes No!—You can find the full text in the Baltimore Sun, Oct. 5, 2001, p. 21A. You'll find other speeches by Congresswoman Lee on her website at http://lee.house.gov.

Dear President Bush—Amber Amundson. Full text of letter at www.ipj-ppj.org/ Reflections%20-%20Advocacy%20Suggestions%20-%20Lesson%20Plans/ Patriotism%20&%20Peacemaking%20IV.htm.

Ashes and Smoke—Words and music by Linda Allen. Recorded by Aurora Chorus, directed by Joan Szymko (concert recording), on *Nightsongs and Lullabies*. Full verson of the song, with additional lyrics by Linda Allen and Marie Eaton, is recorded on Linda Allen's CD, *Where I Stand*.

Singing for our Lives—Holly Near. Recorded on *And Still We Sing: The Outspoken Collection*. Calico Tracks Music, 2002. Audio sample on product page, www.amazon.com.

Interjected lines by Edith Ballantyne, Janet Bruin, and Betty McIntosh. Full context/interview is in *Women for All Seasons,* op cit.

Jane Addams—excerpted from the poem by Gwendolyn Brooks. Full text in *Montgomery and Other Poems*, Third World Press, 2003.